Six Ways to Grow
Houseplants

BY MURIEL ORANS

Countryside
Books

About the Author

Muriel Orans has actively promoted gardening for many years. Since 1963 she has been a member of the Garden Writers Association. Her articles have appeared in many trade magazines, professional journals and newspapers, including the New York Times and the London Times. Mrs. Orans was a prime force in organizing the Indoor Light Gardening Society. She also has been active in the American Horticultural Society, International Geranium Society, and the Association for the Advancement of Science. She has been a guest on Ruth Alampi's garden program on NBC radio and presented an indoor gardening program on the Today Show. She has also served as State Indoor Gardening Chairman for the Oregon State Federation of Garden Clubs.

Mrs. Orans has organized district youth programs for The Federated Garden Clubs. Her interest in youth spilled over into New York public schools where she was the industry coordinator for school gardening. Work pioneered in New York is now being copied in other metropolitan areas across the U.S. She is pre-

sently serving as a member of the Oregon State 4-H Plant Service Committee to help prepare container gardening manuals and programs for urban youth.

Another facet of Mrs. Orans' gardening interest has been research. In 1960 she became a consultant to Brookhaven National Laboratories. During the same year her "Crookneck Report" was published in the Penn State Geranium Manual.

Her first book, **Houseplants and Indoor Landscaping**, was published by Countryside Books in 1973.

About the Photography

Most of the pictures in this book were taken by Arthur Orans, son and partner of Muriel Orans. His horticultural and architectural photo illustrations have been used to illustrate numerous books, magazines and newspaper articles. The Orans photo library now contains well over 10,000 different illustrations.

Orans photographed his subjects with a Leica and accessories.

Other pictures in this book were provided by the following sources.
Acorn Plantqubator - p. 33, right / **American Plywood Association** - p. 9, center left / **Armstrong Cork Company** - p. 12, bottom left; p. 22, left; p. 42, top / **Atlas Asbestos Company** - p. 5, left, top right / **George I. Ball Inc.** - p. 93, top / **Bernard Industries** - p. 36 / **C.D.I.** - p. 25, top left / **California Redwood Association** - p. 9, center right / **Coral Products** - p. 16 / **The Dramm Company** - p. 19 / **E.C.S. Distributors** - p. 25, bottom left / **Environmental Dynamics** - pp. 34-35 / **Evans Products Company** - p. 8; p. 9, bottom; p. 20; p. 21, bottom / **Everlite Aluminum Greenhouses** - p. 41, top; p. 43, bottom left / **Fleco Industries, Inc.** - p. 25, top right / **Floralite Company** - p. 24 / **Georgia-Pacific Corporation** - p. 37 / **The Green House** - p. 26, left / **Henrietta Nursery** - pp. 52-60 / **H.L. Hubbell, Inc.** - p. 26, right / **S.R. Leon** - p. 11; p. 12, right / **Lord and Burnham** - p. 5, bottom right; p. 6; p. 41, bottom left; p. 43, top three, right / **Marko** - p. 25, bottom right / **Mikkelson** - p. 46; p. 47; p. 74; p. 75, top / **Pan American Plant Company** - p. 87, top right, bottom / **Pan American Seed Company** - p. 62, bottom / **Regal Rugs** - p. 9, top / **Small World Ltd.** - p. 33, bottom left / **Sturdibilt** - p. 43, center left / **Vegetable Factory Greenhouses** - p. 40; p. 41, bottom right / **Volkman Bros.** - p. 87, top left / **Window Shade Manufacturers Association** - p. 7, top left; p. 12, top left; p. 13, top

Contents

Introduction

Most houseplanters are eclectic in their acquisition of plants even though many of the plants may not be the best ones for their particular environment. Eventually, the houseplanters wind up with a mixed bag of varieties that are doing fine, barely making it, or as often is the case, progressively on their way out to the garbage heap.

Interior plants and plantings are all part of our life style. Foliage and flowering plants can be found growing in most indoor situations from basement to attic, from air terminal to undercover shopping malls, and from offices to greenhouses. You name the location and you'll find a plant. There are no limits to the kinds of plants you can grow indoors as long as the plant's environmental and cultural requirements are met; yet, under given circumstances, some plants will adapt and perform better than others. No two situations are ever exactly alike, yet many have similarities and, on this premise, we shall endeavor to help you select plants which will live and perform to your satisfaction with a minimum of effort on your part and a minimum of adjustment on the plant's part.

In *Houseplants and Indoor Landscaping,* we illustrated and discussed the environmental and cultural requirements for the tried and true plants that were readily available up to that time and still are. Stress was on the kind of light the plants required for satisfactory maintenance, and suggestions were made about where to grow them indoors.

Recently, the interior pot plant industry became the fastest growing segment of American agriculture. Growing methods have been expanded and improved; new products such as stands, tools and "special" fertilizers have been developed and designed specifically for the indoor gardener. Many plants considered strictly as conservatory subjects have proven adaptable to many interior situations and are now being introduced as "new" plants. Others have been bred specifically for indoor use while others that were primarily hobbyist plants, i.e. Bromeliads, Gesneriads, Cacti and succulents, are now widely available.

Due to the very rapid expansion of the pot plant industry and the kinds of people (many lacking training and experience; who have gone into this "impulse" business, it is often difficult to get adequate, easy-to-understand directions about the selection of a plant, its care and culture, and the different methods and products available to you to aid in developing and enhancing your plants and interior spaces. This is what this book is all about.

We have now reached a point in our green revolution where specialization and limitations on varieties available are determined by the industry's primary objective of rapid turnover. A quick visit to your local florist, commercial greenhouse, supermarket or plant vendor will soon make you aware of this. Every outlet carries exactly the same varieties and pot sizes, and charges about the same price. You will also observe by label, pot and soil mix, that most are grown by the same grower(s) who ship the same plants all over the United States from their vast plantations under glass and/or lath from places such as Florida, California, Puerto Rico and Texas. At this writing apparently anything goes, including barely rooted cuttings, in order to satisfy the public's voracious appetite for green life in their surroundings.

If you want to find and grow plants other than the run of the mill kinds, you'll have to seek them out in some old greenhouse corner, get starts from a friend, join a garden club and/or plant society, grow them from seed, or order your plants as I often do—via mail order catalog.

Most small pot plants, given half a chance, will develop into beautiful subjects that will perform to your satisfaction providing you have given thought to your selection, how to grow it on, and have a place in mind for it at time of purchase. However, this is not often the case—I know— because I too have been guilty of browsing a plant shop, making a purchase because a plant appealed to me, and then wondering where I would grow it. After all, I have just so much window sill space that faces east and south. North and west exposures are fine, but I do prefer the east and south for best growing results. At this writing I don't have an inch of space to spare on any of my sills and it becomes quite a chore to open a window when I want to air through the house. The hanging baskets hooked on over the window frame look beautiful, but only add to the window opening problem. Of course, if you want to use trailing plants in your window instead of curtains this is great—but still you have to open windows once in a while. True, the plants do require light to grow. Natural light, of course, is the least expensive and most energy-saving; yet, there are other methods of providing sufficient light if you want to get away from the dependency of sill light.

Many of the plants available now meet my requirements for good indoor subjects while others do not. You may be sure that all plants and methods I recommend have been put through some very rigid tests. These conclusions should not deter you from trying some that I've found wanting. There just aren't two growing situations exactly alike, and no two people have the same objectives for their plants.

While I find that it is quite impossible for me to grow on indoors a seedling of a cut-leaf Japanese red maple under lights, on a window sill, or in a Wardian case (enclosed fish tank) I've had excellent success with a papaya which is notorious for its poor indoor performance. My next door neighbor who grows most of his material in a lean-to greenhouse has had exactly the opposite result with the aforementioned plants. In fact, he has been able to grow on a maple seedling for at least three years with-

4

Boucherville Shopping Center; Montreal, Canada

This artificial light garden brings beauty and light to an otherwise sober office.

Montreal Airport

5

out it going dormant and has trained it into an exquisite bonsai. Guess you can't win them all.

Once you have made sure that the plant you plan to purchase appears to be vigorous, healthy, clean, pest free and in good form, it should meet the following criteria for your happy houseplanting:

1. The plant should be able to adapt and adjust to the environment it will be placed in, be it window sill, light garden, greenhouse, garden room or other.

2. If selected for a specific situation, i.e. a tropical tree or light garden subject, the plant should be a slow grower yet retain its color and form. Fast growers get out of hand, space and shape and they will either have to be pruned back, repotted or removed—not a happy condition when hundreds of dollars are involved.

3. There should be minimum leaf and flower drop—some plants can be awfully messy, such as the flowering begonias and single floretted geraniums.

4. Avoid the pest inviters. These are plants that actually attract them even through the window screen. Fuschias, *Pelargonium domesticum,* petunias and tomatoes all host white fly; roses host red spider; and mealy bug is most frequently found on succulents and cacti. To avoid some of these pest problems, be sure of your plant sources. Do not be in a rush to accept plants from friends who may be housing said problems with theirs — pests do travel on plants and in the soil.

5. The plant should retain sufficient moisture in stems and leaves so that in the event that you fail to water when needed, it will not collapse, drop leaves or have them become brown margined. Aphelandra and coleus are typical examples of plants that exhibit these negative characteristics.

6. All plants should be compatible in terms of environment and culture when grown together. This means same temperature, light or day length, soil mix, fertilizer and frequency of watering. This is particularly important when growing plants in a controlled situation, such as a light garden or greenhouse. For example, I am now growing in my four tier light garden over fifty different kinds of plants that originated from the four corners of our earth with as many varied climates known to man. Yet, they all appear quite content when exposed to the same conditions and culture—of course, I have developed a few tricks. These will be revealed to you as you delve into this book. All are grown under fluorescent grow lamps with a ten-hour day length that is controlled via timer. Since the light unit serves as a divider between my living room and dining area, we often unplug the timer when we entertain and light the garden. Such upsets in light schedule, in almost a year of growing this way, have shown no adverse effects. When one or two indicator plants, such as the coleus or begonias, begin to droop, all the plants with the exception of the succulents and cacti are water/fertilized thoroughly (watering from the top) with a solution consisting of one capful of fish emulsion to one quart of tepid water. The fertilizer is omitted every fourth session in order to leach through any salts that begin to build up. Other than a bit of grooming, pruning and an occasional half turn of the pots to prevent roots from rooting through the bottom drainage hole into the peagravel bed that the pots sit in, I rarely give my plants much added attention. As for the succulents and cacti, after an initial thorough watering when placed in the light garden, I rarely find it necessary to water them again. It appears that the high humidity released by evaporation of the moisture around the pebbles and the transpiration of the surrounding plants is quite adequate for their needs. Succulents such as the aloes, crassulas and sedums appear to do best for me when set directly on the pebbles, while the cacti prefer to have drier feet. Therefore, I tend to set the cacti atop the

A modern lean-to greenhouse is an excellent place to grow wide variety of plants.

Pelargonium x
hortorum 'Velma'

*This east window is a logical place to
grow and display plants that have
medium light requirements.*

*Author's
room divider light unit.
I've found that plants grown
under lights
for any length of time
have more blue coloration
than green.*

*Saxifraga stolinifera
"Strawberry geranium."
I never did get a chance to grow
the variegated kind
long enough to photograph it.*

soil of one of the plants or balance and suspend them between two pots. Also, I prefer to grow them as window sill
subjects when our natural day length exceeds ten hours
and only resort to a holding action under lights during
our short winter days. Of course, if you are able to have a
greenhouse, lean-to or such where winter temperatures
do not drop below freezing (32°F) you can carry them on
with a minimum of extra heat.

My only experience with failure in trying to grow a
cosmopolitan group of plants in my new light set up has
been with two different plants (from two different
sources) of variegated *Saxifraga stolonifera*. I've yet to
learn their secret needs while for most people they grow
like weeds. Another plant that I've found happier on a
west window sill or in the greenhouse is that most color-
ful geranium *Pelargonium x hortorum 'Velma'*. It needed a greater intensity of light than that available no matter how close up to the light it was grown to bring out
the multi-variegated coloration in its leaves.

7. After selecting a specific plant for a specific place
indoors for a specific purpose and, having grown it for a
year in this specific environment, you should still be able
to maintain its original size, form, vigor and color
without too much effort on your part.

8. All indoor plants you grow should be almost
carefree and perform to your satisfaction without the
need to provide special micro-climates or other conditions. Remember, there are many plants you can enjoy
growing for most interior spaces. There is no need to
struggle with one that just won't or can't make it. Guess
I'll take my own advice and give up on the Saxifraga and
try another plant with similar habit and form such as a
Plectranthus.

To avoid confusion about the identity of plants discussed, all will be labeled with their internationally accepted botanical (Latin) names as well as common
names, which are usually of local origin. A typical example of this is the *Saxifraga stolonifera* known in hor-

ticulture as *Saxifraga sarmentosa* and by the layman as a
"Strawberry begonia" or "Strawberry geranium." This
plant is a Saxifraga and is not even distantly related to a
strawberry, begonia, or geranium. Another example is
the many different kinds of plants known as "Creeping
Charlie". It can be anything from a pilea to a *Nepeta
hederacea* to anything that grows close to the ground
with a creeping habit. Use the correct name for a plant
when ordering from a reliable source and you'll get what
you ordered. I know a semi-commercial grower of
begonias who has most of the plants labeled correctly.
However, if the label is misplaced, the grower re-names
the plant after a friend. Can you imagine the confusion if
you try to get another like any of those from a different
source if it happens to be renamed "Daisy"? Let's learn
to call our plants by their botanical names for easy iden-
tification. You can't go wrong if you seek out a *Cuphea
hyssopifolia*—the plant must have hyssop-like foliage. Or
if the plant's name ends with *albo flora* you will know
that its flowers will be white: albo-white, flora-flower.

*Red geraniums and
a west window are
made for each other.*

Plant Display
Ideas

*The high humidity of the bathroom and
the light available from the greenhouse-type
slanted ceiling help to produce this tropical
bathroom garden. Note how light plants such
as the philodendron and peperomias sit in the
divider shelves at least 10 feet from the
window light source.*

The floor to ceiling north-facing windows of this townhouse living room provide sufficient light to maintain the tubbed Ficus exotica *tree sitting in front of it as well as the* Philodendron x baryi *next to the chair.*

Light, filtered and otherwise, provide the light necessary to maintain and grow these decorative tropicals.

These plants do quite well with a combination of natural and artificial light.

Downlights serve as the sole source of light for these plants.

Window Sill Basics

A Review and Expansion

For a plant to function, you must provide it with a source of light, air, and water. Light is the key to photosynthesis. Without light, plants cannot convert light, air, and water into carbohydrates, proteins and fats for growth. Many plants available today will perform quite satisfactorily on a window sill without the need to create a micro-climate such as is necessary with certain terrarium subjects, which can only exist in a high humidity situation or with plants that do best in a greenhouse where temperatures (day and night), humidity, watering and fertilizing are controlled via clock and thermostat. We shall discuss these situations in later segments.

Window Sill Growing

Since some plants will perform better than others in a given exposure, you will have to experiment a bit to learn which is best for each. Don't be in a rush to shift your plants from one window to another because of some yellowing leaves, bud drop, or die back. Plants, like people, adapt at different rates to new situations—so please be patient. Give them at least three to four weeks of adjustment to their new quarters before considering a move. If however, you observe rapid deterioration within a week look for the cause and not the effect. By this I mean did the plant appear healthy to start with? Was it well rooted? Was it badly handled (dropped or shaken severely) during transport? Or, after a further inspection, is it infested with pests such as mealy bug, white fly, and/or red spider. A poor or non-existent root system, bad handling, and pest infestation are usually the cause for *rapid* deterioration. Too much or too little light, as well as poor watering practices take a much longer time to affect the health and appearance of a plant. A sure sign that your plant(s) have been placed correctly is when you observe signs of new growth and the plant appears to be vigorous with good color.

Select plants in size pots that will sit comfortably on your sill(s) without having plant parts leaning on the glass. Glass is a rapid conductor of heat and cold. Too much of either can cause damage or death to a plant.

When the temperature drops below freezing, glass-touching parts freeze and rot off. You can avoid this, if touch they must, by growing the plants dry during the winter months. Let all the soil go almost completely dry between watering. This will not be harmful to most plants since most are in partial dormancy, with little or no growth evident during the winter months due to the

very short days. If you know that a really deep freeze is forecast, hold off on watering as long as possible until danger is past or, better still, remove the plants from the windows at night when the indoor temperatures drop quickly with the heat loss through the glass. The less turgid the plant is under these circumstances the better, since this cuts down ice crystal formation within the cells, which upon thawing break through the cell walls, causing rotting and eventual loss.

If you are really dedicated to growing plants on sills during the winter, and also interested in cutting down on your heating bills, you can create an insulating layer by lining each window inside with clear plastic. Greenhouse growers have found this quite effective in cutting energy costs without appreciably cutting down the available winter light.

In the summer, with its rapid heat build up and strong penetrating rays, glass touching parts often sunburn (bleach out). Leaves wilt and often become brown margined due to too rapid transpiration.

Most plants do best when grown in a daytime temperature between 65°-75°F and a night time temperature between 55°-65°F. Temperatures 50°F and lower usually stop growth as do temperatures 80°F or higher. I like to keep a thermometer leaning against the glass where I grow plants so that I at least know why certain plants are reacting as they are and, if necessary and possible, I can raise the heat in the house during winter and create a better growing and/or maintenance temperature for them.

As a sill gardener of many many years, I have found the east and south windows suitable for most plants. East and south windows offer a greater year round day length with good strong morning sun that diffuses in the afternoon to a good, strong, steady light until sunset. This is particularly important in the higher latitudes where winter days shorten to seven hours or less and are often overcast and cloudy.

West windows are fine most of the year but should be avoided if possible during the longer days of spring and summer when the sun travels north and is high in the sky. Plants have been known to cook during the late afternoon heat buildup with its accompanying strong, intense light. Plants grown in this kind of environment of 90°F+ may have to be watered twice a day because of the high rate of soil evaporation and plant transpiration. Since I do not have an inch of sill space to spare, I find that to achieve some modicum of relief for my west window plants, I move them to a table away from the window around 4 p.m. when the heat starts to get unbearable, draw the heavy curtains, and wait until sunset before setting them back again. If I know that I'll not be home to perform this service, I place the plants on the table before I leave the house. A day or two with poor light really doesn't affect them too much and it is better than having them cook.

When you have to hold plants for a few days before placing them or if you have plants that prefer or can adapt to a lower light intensity, a north window will suf-

*This north window plant collection seems to be
happy in this kind of light. Plants actually serve as a
privacy curtain for this uncurtained greenhouse-type window.*

Flowering kalanchoes are among the plants brightening up this dining area.

An eclectic plant collection adds interest and variety to this sitting area.

This dining area is enhanced by glass-shelved wicker window dividers that hold an eclectic plant collection.

fice. If these windows are free during the summer, it might be a good idea to move your west window plants to this exposure once the seasonal daylength has advanced to twelve hours.

Too much manhandling is bad for plant or beast, yet recent research indicates that plants that are mildly shaken or rocked, such as when a heavy truck rumbles by or when someone like me walks across a floor or gently bumps into a plant, the plants put down a stronger root system than most while the above ground growth is slowed down. A short period of "rocking" weekly may eventually prove to be a better method of controlling

plant size for space maintenance than pinching and pruning.

Unless you have plans for a specific large specimen such as a tree, shrub, or hanging basket, I suggest that you consider starting out with the smaller sized plants available for economy's sake as well as for the plant's sake. Well-rooted, vigorous, pest-free, small-sized potted plants will adapt faster to interior conditions than the larger plants that have established growing habits. In a sense plants are like people.

There will be little need to adjust water and fertilizer requirements for each plant, since most small-sized pot

This window sill is an excellent example of pebble tray culture.

use under individual plants, I would have to scrub my sills at least once a month and paint them as often as twice a year to prevent rot and unsightly peeling paint. You will note that the trays have almost mocroscopic feet at each corner that lifts the trays just high enough off a level surface to permit air to circulate under and through them and to cut down condensation. If you must grow your plants in glazed ceramics that usually have unglazed bottoms and sweat, it is best to set these atop cork rounds, such as coasters, or glue tiny feet of cork on the bottom to permit air circulation. Believe me, before I learned these tricks, I left a trail of ruined window sills whenever I moved.

Water/fertilizing becomes a no mess, simple operation when plants are grown in the trays or saucers. You can water from top and bottom without having to worry about the water spilling over the tops of the rims of the pots or leaking out the bottom drainage holes. A turkey baster is another handy gadget — it makes an excellent, no drip slurper-upper of the excess standing water that the plant does not take up.

Wet feet can cause many troubles to plants. This often affects their well being when root rot occurs caused by lack of air circulation in the soil. It is best to siphon off all excess water about an hour after you've completed your watering. It is also a good idea to scrutinize your plants thoroughly each time you water. This gives you a chance to check for their condition, pest invasion and grooming. Also give each a half turn so that each forms a well-rounded specimen as it grows. Since I am a lazy gardener—no muss-no fuss, but lots and lots of plants to care for — I prefer to grow all my plants in plastic pots. The rate of evaporation is much slower than clay, therefore watering is not a daily occurrence. Grown in plastic pots and depending on time of year and rate of growth, I find that most of the plants only require a good soak about once a week for satisfactory health and growth. It it better for the soil to be soaked thoroughly each time it is watered rather than by drips and drops. See how to water in *Houseplants and Indoor Landscaping.*

plants come from the same source(s) who grow them in almost identical growing mediums. However, due to their small size (2-inch to 3-inch), you will find that when grown individually they will require frequent watering because the growing medium dries out faster. This may occur more than once a day if the interior atmosphere is dry. To overcome the need for frequent watering, you can create a higher humidity micro-climate just by growing a number of plants close together in a planter such as plastic drawer organizers. Depending on the width of your sills, you can find one or more that sit comfortably at the window. They come in different lengths so that you can find ones that easily hold up to six 2½-inch pots or three 3½-inch pots. There are others that will hold plants grown in 6-inch diameter pots. In addition to serving as leak-proof containers, they also are condensation free underneath, therefore you avoid water marring the sills. Until I found these trays and plastic cereal bowls for

This 9-inch-wide drawer organizer holds four thumb pots or two 3-inch pots. The plants are, left, Pelargonium x hortorum 'Velma', a fancy-leaved geranium, and, right, Pelargonium tomentosum "Peppermint geranium."

This 14-inch-wide kitchen drawer organizer holds five small plants, from left to right, Pilea depressa *"Miniature peperomia";* Senecia herreianus *"Green marble vine";* Pilea *'Moon Valley'; first fronds of a pteris fern "Table fern"; and a blushing young plant of* Strobilanthes dyerianus *"Persian shield."*

*Recycled bottle gardens
in spill-proof drawer organizers*

Onions and scallions in bottle garden

Bottle-gardened sweet potato

Ideas to Ponder

You can't grow plants behind drawn curtains; they need light to live. Plants can be grown more than one pot deep in from the glass. This situation is ideal for lower-level light-requiring plants as well as for many cuttings and plants starting from seed.

Bottle gardens. This kind of garden is especially suited to window sill culture. Plants grown by this method can be both attractive as well as economical and useful. This is also the simplest, cheapest method I know of to increase your collection of plants. Most cuttings from your own plants or those acquired from other sources will root in water, and can either be grown on in water or eventually potted up. Plants grown this way take up less room than those grown in the conventional manner because their root structures are more compact. They don't have to spread out to seek moisture and nutrients since they are all in the solution. I've found this to be the easiest method of holding cuttings and pieces if I don't have the time or inclination to pot them up immediately after a grooming and pruning session. Also, this is the fastest method for rooting up plants that I know of. This method has no limit. It works for succulents as well as other types of plants one grows indoors. In fact, I have better success with this method for succulents than when I pot them up.

Clippings from store-bought scallions and onions grown in water on a kitchen sill can give you months and

14

Cuttings rooting in plastic container

Potted-up cutting of Peperomia obtusifolia

Rooted cuttings of Peperomia obtusifolia
"Baby rubber plant"

Rooted Setcreasea purpurea
"Purple heart" forming a root ball
via the gravel-glass method

months of food flavor. While white and sweet potatoes may not be eaten when grown in water, they do make good, green, lush, fun plants. Try a plant or two; I'm sure you'll enjoy the experience. For best results start with a potato that shows signs of sprouting and without rot. This is one good way of using a potato that becomes inedible because of new growth.

Many plants grown in water can also be grown in a room away from sill light as long as there is some supplemental light. A good example of this is the trailing philodendron that will survive in water almost anywhere indoors. Be sure all foliage is removed from parts that will be sitting in water. Foliage sitting in water has a ten-dency to rot. Rooting usually occurs at the nodes where the leaf and its stem has been removed. Water the plants by keeping the bottle filled to the top rim. About once a month, drop a small eyedropper full of the fish emulsion solution that you use for the regular water/fertilizing into the water. Prune, groom and train as you would any other plant.

If green algae begins to form on the inside of the bottle, leave it alone. I haven't found this harmful to growth. However, if it is aesthetically offensive, remove the plants and scrub out the bottle. Rinse them free of all soap and detergent residue. Start up again with water that has been allowed to sit overnight in a clean container. This is

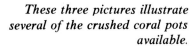

These three pictures illustrate several of the crushed coral pots available.

to permit additives such as chlorine to evaporate and to permit the water to reach room temperature. Really cold water that comes directly from the tap can cool down the plants sufficiently to check their growth.

It is essential that you protect the fine roots that have developed in the water if you want to pot up your plants. A plant with a root ball is always easier to transplant than one that is bare rooted. To overcome this situation, simply set each rooted cutting into its own juice glass or small wide mouthed glass container filled with water. Replace the water by gently pouring gravel into the container until all the water is forced out. Use the kind of gravel prepared for caged birds— I find that this works best. Sand also is fine as long as it is the kind found at river banks. Beach sand with its very high salt content is to be avoided at all costs; this can kill off your plants before you are aware of what is happening. Keep the sand in the container moist at all times. Whenever the top of the sand feels dry to the touch, fill the sand-filled glass with tepid water until it runs over the rim. When roots begin to show on the inside of the glass, you will know that a satisfactory root ball ready for transplanting has been formed. At this time prepare a pot filled with damp growing medium or potting soil that has been hollowed out in the center to fit the glass growing container. The pot should not be much larger than one inch

in diameter than any part of the glass container. Tap out the plant and set its new root ball directly into the hollowed out space. Lightly fill in with soil all empty areas around the sides and top. Water from the top and continue to do so until it begins to seep through the drainage holes. Even under the best of circumstances, transplanting does shock and set back a plant.

Continued on page 18

How to Handle Mail-order Garden Plants

A "Futura" snapdragon

*Upon receipt of your mail-order plants,
open carton immediately.
Remove and unwrap each plant separately.*

A "Sprinter" geranium from seed

*Keep each in its own plastic bag,
so it doesn't dry out too
fast between waterings. Put them
into a kitchen drawer organizer
and set out on sunniest window sill
until outdoor temperature and weather
permit planting into your garden.
This holding-action method
can be applied to all small
mail-order houseplants when
you don't have the time
or inclination to pot them up
immediately on arrival.*

Therefore, for at least three days after transplanting it is best not to set it out directly into a strong light situation. It is better to set it in filtered light, such as one pot in from the window. After the three day period of adjustment if the plant appears to be vigorous, no droop or drop, you can set it in its assigned growing space and let it grow on.

Hanging plants. Windows and hanging plants are made for each other. There is plenty of light and, when given the added space to hang, the plants can grow rampant. You don't have to stick to the usual kinds being offered for sale today but can try to experiment with plants that normally have a spreading habit. Most can be trained to trail over the rim of a planter or will do this on their own. There is no limit to the kinds of hanging containers you can find or devise. Hanging planter containers can be anything from plastic margarine bowls strung with nylon fishing line, with or without drainage holes punched through their bottoms; standard plastic hanging baskets with drip saucers attached and suspended by wire holders, or potted plants set into decorative ceramics (double potting) that do not have any drainage holes. These are usually hung with macrame hangers. For ceramic containers that are designed specifically for hanging plants, leather tongs or nylon fishing line can be tied through the rim holes. Another *method container* that I have found most satisfactory is the new pots made of crushed coral. These are truly a no drip, no over- or under-water pot, (if you follow directions). Until I had the good fortune to acquire some of the remarkable pots, I was most skeptical about their publicity. How can you properly water a plant, particularly a hanging plant, without some water running through the drainage holes, or how can you help but not over-water when there is no drainage? These planters seem to solve these problems as well as the problem of making air available to the soil. If you follow the directions below, I'm sure you'll be as successful with your plants as my friends and I have been.

First, fill the empty pot to the brim with water (no, it won't leak). Let the water absorb through the interior white liner and on through the decorative, crushed-coral exterior. When all parts of the outside feel damp to touch, spill out all the excess water and pot up your plant, making sure that you leave an inch of space between the soil line and the top rim of the pot. This is for all size pots. Fill this inch of space with water (it will absorb down into the soil and begin to evaporate through

when the outside of the pot feels dry to your touch, or if the porous coral) and then hang your plant. Thereafter, water/fertilize with the inch of water procedure only the dipstick (see *Houseplants and Indoor Landscaping)* is moist only one third up from the bottom.

These pots are also excellent for use on sills or for interior use on shelves, tables, plant stands, or the floor. Because each planter comes with its own set of tiny cork feet, there are no water marring problems. These feet lift the container up high enough off a surface to permit enough air circulation under the pot so that bottom moisture evaporates before it gets a chance to accumulate.

Water/fertilizing hanging plants can get quite messy. The simplest method of course is to carry each to a sink or tub and give the soil a thorough soak. This means until the water begins to dribble through the bottom drainage holes. Then let all the excess water drain off (until it stops dripping) before hanging the plant back at the window. If you are "blind" watering, that is if a plant is double potted into a ceramic or plastic decorative container that does not have drainage holes, siphon off all excess water that accumulates at the bottom of the outer pot before returning the plant to its growing space.

The "removal" method can become quite a chore and mess especially if you have to move some of those tremendous fern specimens. A ladder is a must if you plan to bring the water/fertilizer to your plants. It is best to stand up to your plant. To do a good clean job, use a siphon-type wand that takes up fluid through a hose set in a pail of water or a long necked watering can. In any case you'll have to water judiciously— that is to water thoroughly without dripping or spills. Each time you water, water thoroughly so that the soil is evenly damp from the bottom of the pot through to the top. If in doubt about when to water, use the dipstick method. Most plants are content to wait until the stick is moist only one third up from the bottom of the pot. Of course there are always exceptions, such as the Episcias I grow. They prefer a constantly moist yet thoroughly drained soil. No wet feet for them or they will soon rot and die or curl up when dry.

If you grow your hanging plants outdoors during the summer or where the climate warrants, water as often as required. Use your regular garden wand soaker; it does a thorough, efficient job. To compensate for the lack of fertilizer in the water, water/fertilize weakly weekly via watering can.

The WAND method of watering hanging plants

*Decorator lamp next to
Philodendron oxycardium
"Heart Leaf Philodendron"
helps provide necessary light.*

Windowless Gardening

Many large tropical and sub-tropical trees, shrubs and plants, such as the palms, polyscias and peperomias, will adapt indoors to much lower light intensities than they are accustomed to in their natural habitat. Unless you grow your plants in a greenhouse, you will rarely be able to produce the enormous, robust specimens that can be found growing outdoors in the Florida and California landscapes. You may even be hard put to recognize some of these plants as those kinds that you are presently growing indoors. Sunlight, air, day length, and un-confined roots permit the plants to develop to their fullest form and color.

If you prefer to keep your sills clean and clear or if you have a certain interior space that just needs that "green" accent to complete your decor, choose plants that will perform best in medium to low light. (See *Houseplants and Indoor Landscaping.*) Purchase

these from a source that is known to "harden off" their plants. This means that Florida or California field-grown or lathe-house-grown plants have been grown on for at least three months in average interior light and temperatures before being offered for public sale. Although the initial expense for this kind of material will be higher, you will be sure that your plants, particularly the large expensive specimens, will adapt faster and retain the form and color that you were so careful to select.

I suggest that medium light requiring plants (hanging, table or floor) be grown no further than five feet into a room if it is to depend primarily on available window light for maintenance. For those plants that can adapt to low light situations, I would limit their placement to no more than ten feet in from a natural light source. This goes with the premise that at certain

The plant in the middle is a Crassula argentea *"Jade plant." The rest are, from left to right,* Nephrolepis exaltata *'Fluffy Ruffles' (the first two plants);* Sansevieria trifasciata laurentii *"Variegated snake plant";* Nephrolepis exaltata biserrata *"Bold sword fern."*

times of day artificial light will be used to further light the room, and/or curtains and drapes will be kept open during the daytime to make use of all available natural light.

Certain plants such as a *Sequoia sempervirens* burl, *Spathiphyllum 'Mauna Loa',* and the well known *Schlumbergera bridgesii* "Christmas cactus" all grow beautifully for me two to three feet from a drape drawn west window. There are probably many different kinds of plants that will perform as well. Experiment by trying a few on your own.

The Sequoia sits atop a thin layer of peat moss in a copper pan. It is kept constantly wet by maintaining water almost up to the rim of the container. A regular fertilizer solution is used almost daily to replace the moisture that evaporates or that which the plant takes up for its own use.

The *Spathiphyllum 'Mauna Loa'* is thoroughly water/fertilized only when the dipstick is moist about half way up from the bottom.

As for the *Schlumbergera bridgesii,* it rarely has to be water/fertilized more than once a month. This occurs only when the soil becomes completely dry and the new

Monstera deliciosa *"Split leaf philodendron" with downlight*

growing tips begin to show signs of wilting; rarely requiring more than a half cup of water/fertilizer per session; quite often less, because when I go back to check for over-watering, I usually have to remove about a tablespoon of fluid from the saucer. Like any true epiphyte (a plant with a very small root system that lives on another plant without being a parasite) it appears to get most of its nutrients and water directly from the air. Also like many other epiphytes, such as certain orchids, bromeliads and ferns which grow bare root in trees, the schlumbergera adapts quite readily to pot plant culture. Contrary to most cultural information about how to bloom this variety, my plant, as it is grown, produces sparse bloom most of the year and is overladen with blossoms around Christmas time. Unfortunately, we could not photograph it in all its color. It seems that prolonged exposure to the photo flood lamps we use caused all the blossoms to wilt and pop off. With or without blossoms, it does make a decorative plant that has an interesting form and growing habit.

The use of available natural or artificial light for plant growth and maintenance is the cheapest method I know of. I mean the kind of natural light that comes through a window or the kind of lights that are kept on continually for from ten to twelve hours daily in enclosed commercial spaces, such as offices, waiting rooms, and hotel lobbies. If you do not have a minimum of a ten hour day length in your latitude, you will find it necessary to supplement the daylight with artificial light during the shorter days of winter to extend the day length to at least ten hours. This is the shortest period I know of to grow and/or bloom most plants satisfactorily that are presently available to the public. For the larger free-standing tree-like forms, you can use down-light spot lamps installed with incandescent grow lights or any of the many incandescent lights presently available that have a flat, silvered surface. Just be sure that they are not so close to the top of a plant that the heat radiating from the lamp will burn the top foliage. True, the closer the light to a plant, the more intensity there is available to it. The hand test may help you determine the correct distance from the plant. With palm facing down about six inches from the light source, lower it until the heat feels comfortable—about as lukewarm as the milk in a baby's bottle. Hanging plants suspended below this kind of light grow quite well. Another method of offering overhead light is via "track lights" with spot lamps that can be moved across the ceiling to focus on a particular plant.

A table plant such as a small peperomia, philodendron or even "African violet" will be quite content to grow in light made available to it from a close by floor lamp or decorator lamp sitting with it.

Tropicals
Familiar as Houseplants . . .

Brassia actinophylla *"Schefflera"*
indoor version

Brassia actinophylla *"Schefflera"*
outdoor version

22

That Have Adapted to Indoor Culture

Shown here in outdoor settings

Ficus decora *"Rubber plant"*

Philodendron selloum
"Lacy tree philodendron"

Dracaena draco *"Dragon tree"*

Agave attenuata *"Dragon tree agave"*

*Front row — various sedums; Aloe arboescens
"Candelabra aloe" (red/orange flowers);
Crassula argenta "Jade plant" (white flowers).
Back row — Lemon Tree; Crape Myrtle.*

Artificial Light Gardening

Where winter light intensity is poor and the day length is shorter than nine hours, you may find it expedient to grow your plants by the artificial light gardening method. You can use this method for year around growing, or only restrict your plants to this method during the short days of winter and then return them to their natural light environment when the day length again reaches at least nine hours. The major advantage to growing your plants in a light garden is that you can successfully grow and even bloom plants if you wish in the darkest corner or closet.

There aren't any big secrets about how to grow under lights, particularly if you plan to grow a mixed compatible collection for your own and your guests' pleasure. If you just keep in mind that growing plants under light is merely a substitute for natural light/window sill gardening, the bugaboo of complexity will vanish. All the rules for growing happy, healthy plants apply.

Depending on the number and sizes of plants you grow, a light unit can be as small and inexpensive as a setup with a twenty-watt eighteen-inch fluorescent tube, or as large as the giant package with tier on tier of eight-foot-long units and shelves that go as high as your ceiling permits. If you wish to keep costs down and/or have a special space you want to light, build your own light garden by assembling and constructing the parts, such as light fixtures, tubes, shelves, timer, and trays. The construct-your-own method was what most early artificial growers had to practice because until the early 1960's so called commercially manufactured units were not available. Now, with the greatly expanded interest in green indoors and the public's awareness that you can substitute artificial light for natural light, manufacturers have found it worthwhile to produce a wide variety of units to meet the demand. Many will even "special order" a unit to meet your requirements.

Since your objective is to grow beautiful plants, you will have to concern yourself with the kind of light and intensity that will be advantageous to the majority of your plants. From past and present experience, I have found that a combination of one cool white to one warm white fluorescent tube works almost as well as the specially engineered grow lights that give off a minimum of visible colored light. The lamps with low visible color, such as the Luxor power twist tubes by Dura-Test, are less disturbing when you have to look at them and your plants than those that give off a violet to rose-pink hue. These power twist tubes give off 30% more light that is closest to natural light at no added energy cost.

Light unit for table or floor filled with newly-received miniature roses

Many different plants can be grown together and maintained satisfactorily in a day length of ten hours. Anything less tends to spindly growth, poor color and poor show of flowers. For average growing, lights suspended eighteen inches above the growing shelf work fine for most plants. Also, this arrangement makes it easier to see into and enjoy your plants than if the lights are kept lower. The closer the plants are to the lights, the higher the available light intensity (foot candles). Also, the intensity is found to be higher towards the centers of the tubes than it is at the ends. Based on this information, you can place plants with the higher light requirements towards the center of the unit(s) and others with the lower light requirements towards the ends of the tubes. You

*Ideally suited to hanging basket culture
in the darkest spaces, these "Life Lites"
have an incandescent "grolamp"
in the upper ceramic bowl.*

*This well-designed artificial light garden
is also a useful bookcase.*

Custom-made two-tier unit.

*This artificial light garden
is an attractive addition
to wall unit book shelves.*

This GRO-CART provides ideal conditions for a wide variety of plants.

can usually tell if a plant is properly placed when it shows good color, retains its form, does not stretch or tend to grow to one side (lean), and regularly puts out new strong growth. It may even start to bloom and then continue to do so. Too high an intensity (too much is as bad as too little) is indicated when the foliage begins to curl under, clasps its leaves down close to its pot (African violets do this) and gives the general appearance of shrinking away from the light. Move plants so affected towards the ends of the tubes. Or, if you are growing a whole shelf of plants that react this way, you may find it necessary to raise up the light unit two inches or more away from the plants.

Do not concern yourself if your plants, particularly the foliage kinds, develop strange colors and compact growth when grown under fluorescent lights. They are perfectly healthy and are merely adapting to a higher light intensity than they had been accustomed to in a previous growing place. Plants with insufficient light often will send out very large pale spindly growth to expose as much surface area as possible to any light source as it reaches out. You may have seen this happening to your geraniums, impatiens and coleus when you winter them over indoors or on a window sill. If this occurs cut them back down to the last three leaves or nodes (the place from where the leaves and branches grow) and, if you have the space, set them into your light garden. Even the low light strength areas are better than short day length sill light because the light is constant rather than changing from sunrise to sunset and from overcast, snow, rain, or weak winter sunlight.

I know of no correct universal combination of lights or intensity strengths for all plants. Optimum light and cultural conditions vary from one variety to another in the same genus (relative) and often from clone to clone (cuttings propagated from the same stock plant that basically have the same characteristics with the same variation). For example, the *Aloe variegata ausana* "Tiger aloe" "Partridge-breast" is quite content to be grown near the ends of the tubes. Growth is slowed down,

A piece of elegant living room furniture can hide all the apparatus for an artificial light garden.

A mini-landscape adds interest to this artificial light garden.

My four-tier unit with the valences up

but in no other way is the plant affected. However, its "kissing cousin" *Aloe aristata* "Lace aloe" shows definite signs of preference for sitting smack in the middle of the growing shelf to keep its well rounded, balanced shape. I've grown plants of this particular variety under different conditions for at least twenty years and can vouch for their preference. Grown correctly to specimen size of at least eight inches in diameter shaped in a well-balanced round rosette, it is sure to earn a blue ribbon when placed in competition. It is much easier to produce this kind of plant under lights than if you have to grow it on a window sill — I know, I've done it both ways and won my ribbons.

As for clonal differences and preferences, they may best be understood by my recent experiences with plants of *Begonia sempervirens albo-foliis* "Calla begonia" Never an easy plant to grow, I gave this up years ago as one of my lost causes until I tried it under lights. Now I have one plant that grows so full and lush that it requires pinching (pruning) back as often as once a month to keep it confined to its consigned space. Its sister cutting taken at the same time from the same stock plant, rooted in exactly the same way side by side in the same glass of water, potted up in the same growing medium and placed in exactly the same light situation just didn't make any growth to speak of for the first three months. In fact it kept dropping as many leaves as it produced. As a last resort, before dumping it, I moved it to my nursery shelf giving it same placement as it had in the regular display shelf. Within two weeks, it started to take off and is now fast catching up with its more robust sister. The nursery shelf is the top-most tier of a four shelf unit that I use as a room divider. The lights are only twelve inches above the growing shelf rather than the usual eighteen inches. Also, with heat rising up from the lower three tiers the temperature is at least 5°F higher than the

Same unit with the valences down

others. I feel that the additional heat and light intensity may be the factors in getting this particular "clone" to take off.

The nursery shelf is exactly what the name implies. This is where I start young plants from cuttings, germinate plants from seeds, and hold plants pot on pot for gifting or for a club project, such as supplying small plants to children living at the local orphanage or as tray favors to nursing home residents. Since most of these plants are small and move out of the garden at a brisk pace, I do not concern myself with providing good air circulation around the plants.

A constant exchange of air both down into the soil and around the plant is essential for good culture. You have to compensate for this lack when growing under lights. This can be done very simply by giving each plant sufficient growing space around it so that it does not touch its neighbors. This method also permits light to reach all parts of each plant without having to contend with shadows cast on each other. You can see this happening in a forest where closely grown trees battle with each other for the light and space above the main tree cover as it cuts down the light on the forest floor with its widespread green umbrella.

The method of growing plants in the shelves set in soldierly lines may be fine for units placed in a basement or attic where they are not in constant public view. My preference is to create a mini-landscape consisting of a variety of plants, driftwood, rocks and sculptures. It can offer the feeling of a jungle or the restricted mood of a Japanese landscape. It can have plants that trail over the sides or a combination of all forms. My own room divider four-tier unit with its different gardens serves as the primary area of interest for my living room decor. To overcome the distraction of having to look up into the lights of the upper two tiers when entertaining, I've devised and had installed valances that flip down to conceal the lights. Otherwise, they are in the up position to permit adequate air circulation.

Date palm seedling, seed, and bare rooted seedling

Light Gardening Hints

Your initial unit should always be twice as large as you think you'll need. At first you may find the space under an eighteen-inch, two-tube unit adequate but with added growth and added plants you will soon be looking for more "lighted" space. After taking a local census of what people have done with their first, small unit I find that most have been replaced with the larger kinds consisting of at least two tiers. The original unit is either stored away in some closet or, as one friend did, set up on a shelf in the basement for use in the winter time to carry over some cuttings of garden geraniums. Another friend uses it to push a special plant or two for exhibition and competition. Depending on the kind of plant she plans to enter, she will place them under the lights anywhere from two to three months before showing and sets them on a continuous light schedule— by keeping them lighted round the clock. This plus water/fertilizing them on demand, grooming and shaping all contribute to the production of magnificent prize winning specimens.

Each unit should contain a minimum bank of two tubes— four tubes are even better and give you a greater concentration of light for almost the same energy costs. Multi-tier units should be wired separately; then each can be plugged into a master socket. This permits you to pull the plug on a unit not in use and save some energy and money.

A timer is a must even for the smallest unit or those in a decorative piece of furniture. This will save you time and energy and assure your plants light even when you oversleep or are away for a few days.

Trays for containing your plants can be of any material that is waterproof, such as plastic, glass, metal or wood, and has a depth of at least one half inch. For safety sake and for easy housekeeping, line each with heavy duty plastic in such a way that it comes up to the rim of the tray.

Drainage is provided by lining the trays to a depth of at least one quarter inch with the following: pea gravel, sand, perlite or a sheet of plastic waffle board— the kind usually used to conceal fluorescent fixtures in offices, etc. I prefer to use either the pea gravel or the waffle board because they do not compact, can be washed clean after heavy use and then be reused.

When after thoroughly water/fertilizing each plant from the top, you note that the water level in the trays is higher than the drainage material, slurp up as much as you can with your trusty turkey baster. No plant or person likes to have constantly wet feet.

For convenience sake, try to get your plants to adapt to a weekly water/fertilizing schedule. For best results start all of them together at the same time with a thoroughly soaked growing medium.

A good kind of growing medium for artificial light gardening culture should contain a substance, such as perlite, which holds moisture yet permits good air movement around each particle. A good all-purpose growing medium should consist of by volume a mixture of three parts commercial potting soil, three parts horticultural perlite and one part bird gravel. All of these products can be found packaged in places such as supermarkets, florists, and garden centers. I prefer to use this mix for all my gardening. It really works for everything from terrarium culture to potting up cacti and succulents. Since I don't grow orchids, I really can't advise this mix for them.

Grow all-of-a-kind nursery shelf plants together in individual drawer organizers and line them up alongside each other. The one-sided overlapping lips make this an easy way of holding a whole line up of trays that will not take up more space than is necessary to place them out on the shelf.

If you grow by variety rather than by a mixture of small plants, you can water each section by demand. Almost like human babies they will do best on this kind of non-schedule. On-demand watering for young plants grown in small pots such as in the nursery means you water when the dipstick indicates damp one half the way up from the bottom—or in the case of plants such as coleus, when you observe the leaves drooping. In any event it is a good idea to check out the soil every other day by feeling it with your fingers. You'll soon get to know when there is rapid drying out; when in doubt consult the dipstick to confirm your conclusions. For example cacti and succulent seedlings may only require water once a month because the soil must be permitted to go completely dry between waterings; otherwise expect to lose a lot of them due to rot-out caused by too much moisture. Other kinds of seedlings and cuttings may require a thorough watering as often as every other day until they are thoroughly rooted (when you see root hairs peeping through the drainage holes at the bottom of the pot) and are ready to be shifted up into larger pots for placement in the regular display shelves or given away as gifts.

If you plan to start some out-of-the-ordinary plants such as papaya, dates, grapefruit, apples, and ginko from seeds, you may find the best procedure is to plant two seeds of a kind into each thumb pot filled with thoroughly moistened growing medium and to slip a plastic bag over the drawer filled with these pots before setting it up into the nursery. This warm, high humidity, closed environment will force germination faster than any other method I know. Also, it cuts down the need for frequent watering. Only after the seeds germinate (start to grow) are you to remove the plastic cover. It is at this time when you will have to start watering on demand.

Under all circumstances both in and out of the light garden, be sure that each time a plant is watered the growing medium is thoroughly soaked through and that all standing water is removed as soon as possible after watering.

Curtain your units with clear plastic to keep dust from accumulating on your plants (the heat thrown off from the light tubes attracts it) and to maintain a higher humidity than that existing in the room. Attach the curtains in such a way that they can be quickly rolled up and/or removed for viewing, watering and grooming. This curtain method is particularly good for air con-

Papaya is a natural for bonsai because it dwarfs easily and foliage reduces in scale when root growth is restricted.

ditioned rooms where the humidity is constantly being wrung out of the air; or in a spare room where the heat is kept at minimum during the cold months of winter.

In a situation where the summer heat buildup in a room becomes too unbearable for you and your plants, you can either air condition, use a fan to circulate the air or do as I do to compensate for the extra heat given off by the light units. I simply reverse the day for the plants. I light them during the coolest part of the day and instead of having my lights go on at 8:00 a.m. and off at 6:00 p.m., I reset my timer in reverse so that it goes on at 8:00 p.m. and off at 6:00 a.m. This does not seem to affect the plants one iota.

Another energy saving method is to reverse the heating of rooms you use and grow your plants in. We do it and find our energy bills are always lower than our friends and neighbors. Since we are not home during most of the day, we keep the thermostats set as low as 55°F and in the evening and through the night move it up to a comfortable living temperature. I've practiced this method for at least twenty years and have found that we are less prone to colds and my plants do just as well as they would under normally accepted heating. This method even works for sill-grown plants. In fact it was because I started out doing this to a geranium collection I was growing that I was able to come up with this goody.

I prefer to use standard plastic pots for growing all my plants because they do not dry out as fast as the other kinds and can be easily washed up for reuse. However, if I do happen to run out of the smaller sizes and am in a rush to pot up a young plant out of its small starter pot, I will resort to practically any kind of container. The white styrofoam coffee cups are inexpensive and an ideal substitute. To make sure of adequate drainage, I simply punch the tines of a fork through the bottom.

For the record, label your plants. A plant label, in addition to serving as a dipstick, can also hold a vast amount of very pertinent information such as name, date purchased or propagated, when repotted, etc. In the case of seeds: when planted, date germinated and date shifted to growing pot. If you know that a grapefruit seed takes about four weeks to germinate and that corn takes as little as three days, you may not be in a rush to dump the grapefruit seeded pot if it doesn't show green for at least five weeks after you planted it.

If you find that a particular plant in your mini-landscape is performing poorly because its low growing habit cuts down on the amount of light intensity that reaches it, you can compensate for this situation by either raising the plant up by setting it atop a plastic container so that it can get closer to the kind of light it needs or replace it with another kind of plant of similar habit that requires or will adapt satisfactorily to a lower light intensity environment.

I recently encountered this situation with an *Episcia cuperata 'Silver Sheen'*. There it sat week after week just holding on and not even sending out a new leaf. Only after reading an article about light requirements for its plant family in a garden magazine did I realize how inadequate the light was where I was growing it. Within just a week after raising it high enough so that its topmost leaves were about four inches from the light, it started off in all directions and began to bloom within six weeks and continued to do so without let up. All members of its family make excellent light garden subjects because in addition to a good source of light they also prefer a relative humidity of at least 50°F or higher and to be grown warm in a temperature of from 65°F to 75°F and even higher. They are cold sensitive so be sure to use tepid solution when watering.

Pests such as white fly, red spider, aphids and houseflies can become quite a nuisance if only to look at. A few simple methods of control are: get rid of the plants they congregate on. Most pests have special preferences and will not settle for anything else. Plants such as the *Pelargonium domesticums* "Martha Washington geranium" are notorious hosts for white fly, and miniature roses are a natural attractant to red spider. I've often seen them web up a plant overnight.

To avoid pest infestations and disease, try not to bring cut garden flowers into the same room that you grow your indoor plants. Even though the flowers appear to be pest and disease free, you'd be amazed at what they can transport and then have descend on your sitting duck plants. These can include any or all of the following: Red spider, aphids, scale, white fly, house fly, mealy bug, fungus, blight and powdery mildew. Florists' flowers are usually safe since most come from pest- and disease-controlled greenhouses.

You can also join the pests as a hobbyist friend does in his orchid greenhouse. He keeps a few tomato plants growing year round in with his orchid plants. You'll always see masses of very active white fly on these, yet an orchid plant grown up close to the tomatoes never shows any sign of white fly. To tell the truth, I was quite reluctant to accept a gift plant out of his greenhouse but couldn't refuse. Even though white flies were swarming around us as we left the greenhouse I noted that there were none on the plant and, after a careful scrutinizing when I arrived home, I felt it safe to place the plant among my own.

Another method that I've found to work at the beginnings of an infestation is to spray all plants with a caged bird miticide. This spray is safe for man, plant, and beast.

Still another comparatively safe method is to suspend a "Shell No Pest Strip" to one side of the unit out of the reach of children and birds. Yes, I still have my two parakeets flying free most of the time. (See *Houseplants and Indoor Landscaping.*)

Housekeeping in the light garden should be as constant as each time you water. Leaves and other debris left too long atop the soil or on the growing bed will rot out and invite fungii that can often be as destructive to your plants as some pests. Keep your garden clean, and your plants will show their appreciation by growing beautifully for you.

If you are interested in delving into the technical aspects of growing under lights or how to grow a specific family of plants (such as Begonias, Orchids and Gloxinias), under lights join a plant society. Their bulletins are always filled with information about their particular specialty. For information write to:

Indoor Light Gardening Society
c/o Mrs. James C. Martin
423 Powell Drive
Bay Village, Ohio 44140
Dues $5.00 per yr.

The African Violet Society of America Inc.
P.O. Box 1326
Knoxville, Tennessee 37901
Dues $6.00 per yr.

The American Gloxinia and Gesneriad Society Inc.
c/o Mrs. William Rowe
Box 174
New Milford, Conn. 06776
Dues $7.00 per yr.

International Geranium Society
11960 Pascal Ave.
Colton, Ca. 92324
Dues $5.00 per yr.

American Orchid Society Inc.
Botanical Museum of Harvard University
Cambridge, Mass. 02138
Dues $12.50 per yr.

Hydroponic Gardening

Above   *Margarine container is the water/fertilizer source with a hole cut through the cover.*

Right   *A wicked plant.*
The shield under the leaves
is cut from a plastic cover
and is used to prevent leaves from
leaning on the rim of the growing pot
and becoming disfigured.

Hydroponic culture is a soilless method of gardening that uses inert matter, such as sand, gravel or cinders, as a substitute for the soil that serves as a means of supporting the plant and as a medium for making nutrients available to the roots. Hydroponic gardening today is an applied method devised about one hundred years ago by scientists to determine the different kinds and amounts of chemicals (nutrients) that plants require for maintenance and growth. This is still an on-going project all over the world to enable food short nations to grow crops where the land is agriculturally unsuitable, such as certain areas in Africa and Asia.

Recent research indicates that plants require certain essential elements (nitrogen, phosphorous, potassium, carbon, hydrogen and oxygen) as well as a growing list of micro-elements (calcium, magnesium, sodium, sulphur, iron, manganese, zinc, copper, molybdenum, boron, and chlorine) for optimum growth and production. For plants to utilize these, the elements must be made available to the roots in their simplest chemical form and in solution.

Interior gardeners, including those who garden in greenhouses, have found that this scientific method is easily applied to their own kind of gardening. This method of gardening indoors is particularly appealing if you are the kind of person who loves to travel yet loves your plants enough so that your excursions are limited to the length of time available between essential watering. Plant sitters are fine, but somehow your plants become aware of a change of touch and usually react negatively.

The application, by the layman, of most scientific research is an every day occurrence. Therefore don't let the word *hydroponic* put you off. This method of gardening is no more complicated than those conventionally used.

Hydroponic Gardening on a Small Scale

The nutrient solution is nothing more than an all-purpose water soluble fertilizer that contains all the essential elements as well as the micro-elements. Read the label on the container to check out this kind of information. The source for the element can be chemical or a combination of chemical and organic.

Use only one half the recommended amount of fertilizer on the package when mixing up a batch of nutrient solution. For convenience sake mix up at least twice as much as you need for a single treatment. It's always good to have some extra on hand for tipping emergencies or above average absorption and transpiration caused by either high heat, low humidity, or a combination of both.

The nutrient is transferred from the container with the solution in it to the container with your plant in it by a wick. Use a wick long enough so that when it is inserted through the bottom of the drainage hole and fastened inside with a loose knot, it is long enough to reach down to the bottom of the nutrient tank with enough to spare to encircle the bottom. The nutrient tank can be simple as a clean, covered margarine bowl with a hole punched through the top so that a wick can be slipped through the hole. Have the potted plant sit atop the cover so that the wick is the only part in contact with the solution. Any variation of this application should work. Many "African violet" growers find this method of wicking for plants grown in either the inert or conventional growing mediums gives them better results than those grown and watered by the usual methods.

The following all make excellent man-made wicks: braided rope made up from strips cut from old nylon stockings, or pieces of fiberglass cord or strips cut from a new nationally available product called CAP-MAT—a capillary matting made up of long lasting nylon. I haven't used this new product in mat form, but all reports I've gotten so far indicate that it makes an excellent substitute for sand in capillary water systems as applied to plant benches for greenhouse growing.

The natural method of wicking is based on the idea that once a plant becomes root bound (roots fill up the entire pot), they begin to grow out through the bottom of the pot. Rather than repot the plant, have the roots serve as a wick. This is done by setting the potted plant atop the same kind of tank we just described and permitting the roots to reach down through the hole and on into the solution. You can grow plants by this method without having to repot them as long as they do not grow so large that they become top heavy and tend to tip.

For the interior gardener who is primarily interested in growing beautiful plants there are many advantages to hydroponic gardening. Since the supportive medium is inert (lacking in active properties), there is little chance of exposing your plants to unsterilized soil-bearing pests and diseases. For those who spend a

These plants are being grown via the wicking method in the east window of our den.

great deal of time away from home yet want to grow plants indoors, the wicking and/or root wicking method typical of this culture will permit you to stay away as long as the nutrient container has some of the solution. Or, if you plan a vacation longer than you know it takes to empty the container, play it safe and substitute it with a much larger one. For example why not substitute the usual margarine container that looks so pretty with a tall, narrow, plastic quart container that usually comes filled with cottage cheese or ice cream. Or, if this is not feasible, place the plants on a table close to a window that either has its curtains (see

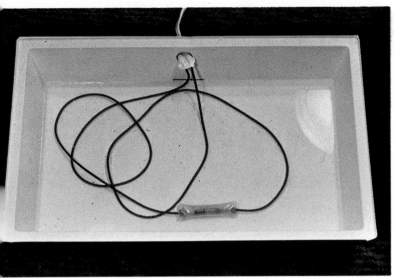

Waterproof heating cord in solution tray keeps the solution at a minimum of 70 for best germination and growth.

Plastic egg crate planter removed from growing solution illustrates wicks and bare roots.

Growing a mini-vegetable garden indoors using CAP-MAT wicks

through) drawn or blinds partially closed. This is particularly important in the summertime when there is usually heavy heat build up and poor air circulation in a closed up vacationer's home.

From my own experience, I've found that hydroponically grown plants often have a smaller, more compact root system because of the easy availability of the nutrients as they are washed through the pea gravel-filled pots that I grow some of my plants in. Also once all the excess standing solution is removed, the roots can still obtain nourishment from the tiny moisture beads that cling to the pea gravel. Since only some of my plants are wicked, I find that those that are not, do require more frequent nutrient flushing than those same varieties grown in my regular growing medium. For those such as the "African violets" that are on a constant water/fertilizing program, I find that a once-a-week replacement of used up nutrient solution is all that they require. The growth for both wicked and unwicked plants is constant because the basic essentials in the nutrient solution are constant. The few disadvantages such as having to clean up spills from tipped nutrient containers are more than compensated for by this very simple gardening method.

Hydroponic Gardening on a Large Scale

Hydroponic gardening in a greenhouse, in a basement set up with banks of artificial lights or in outdoor beds where seasonal temperatures are adequate may prove to be a cheaper means of bringing in a crop, especially certain vegetables (tomatoes, cucumbers, peppers, etc.) than that normally practiced by gardeners and commercial growers. This is because both the water and nutrients are recycled more than once through the growing medium rather than being lost after each water/fertilizing by regular draining off.

The simplest approach to larger scale hydroponic gardening is to fill water-proof growing beds with at least eight inches of gravel, cinders, or crushed stone. There should be a drainage hole at one end of the bed covered with a fine wire mesh (to prevent clogging) to which a collecting hose is attached and to this a pump that pumps back up the unused nutrient solution into the holding tank via another hose. The beds can be any dimension that fits into the space(s) you plan to use. A holding tank filled with nutrient solution should be placed close enough to the bed(s) and be high enough so that the solution flows down into the bed thoroughly flushing the growing medium, and then is retrieved by pumping it back into the holding tank. This can be a totally automated procedure that flushes and retrieves on a twice daily schedule — or more when the crop warrants — or this can be done manually by you. Food plants grown by this method have exactly the same nutritional value and their flavor and appearance are the same of better than those grown in the usual way.

Greenhouse gardeners who have installed a totally automated system report that this is a lazy man's method of simple clean growing and the perfect solution for releasing the strings that can tie you to a daily watering schedule. With automation, you can pick up and get away from home for two or more weeks without having to depend on a greenhouse sitter. An occasional check by a friendly neighbor to see that all is functioning properly should be sufficient.

If you prefer manufactured rather than do-it-yourself equipment, you can obtain excellent materials from redwood benches to specially designed greenhouses from certain suppliers who are into hydroponic gardening in a big way.

Three firms worth investigating are:

> Environmental Dynamics
> P.O. Box 996
> Sunnymead, California 92388
>
> Continental Nutriculture Company
> Box 6751
> Lubbock, Texas 79413
>
> Burwell Geoponics Corporation
> Box 125
> Rancho Santa Fe, California 92067

Each offers a catalog that in addition to offering all kinds of supplies is also filled with pertinent information to assist in the enjoyment of growing plants hydroponically.

The building in this photo is one kind used for large-scale hydroponic gardening.

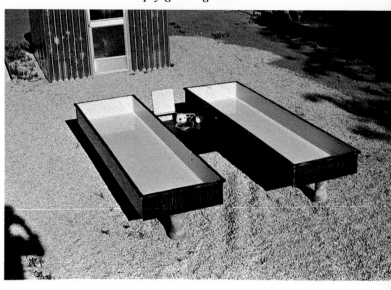

Empty growing beds

*Growing beds with recently
transplanted
tomato plants*

The tomatoes begin to grow

. . . and grow . .

. . . and grow . . .

. . . and ripen.

*Note the smaller containers being used
for hydroponic gardening.*

Terrariums

Terrariums make excellent window sill subjects as well as subjects for interior spaces as long as there is sufficient light for maintenance and growth. A terrarium is a *covered,* glass-enclosed garden that provides a total environment for the plant(s) grown in it. If the container for growing plants is used without a cover the garden is then considered a dish garden.

Although many authors advise that the top should be opened only once in three months for a fresh air exchange, I have had excellent results lifting off the covers as often as once a week. I find that this cuts down on the growth of green algae. In any event, my covers never make a complete seal so there is always some air interchange.

Although ideally suited for the growing of high-humidity-loving plants, you'd be amazed by the fact that some of my most successful experiences have been with low-humidity-requirement succulents such as *Kalanchoe pinnata* "Air plant". It just happened that I was given three tiny plantlets (they form on the outer margins of the mature leaves) at just about the time I was preparing a wine bottle terrarium for photography. I dropped the plantlets down through the thin bottle neck and let them lay where they dropped, never even bothering to tamp them down into the soil. Now, four months later, each plantlet has developed into a mature plant with plantlets beginning to form around the leaf margin. If this kind of growth continues much longer, I shall soon be seeing this bottle completely filled with greenery, making an effort to climb out of its bottle. Try something different — you too may come up with something unusual.

The liquor and wine bottles I recycle as terrariums come from digging through the piles at our local recycling center. They are just as attractive and serve the same purpose as those you can buy commercially. The only drawback I find is that you have to deal with very narrow necks. Planting through these narrow necks can be tricky but the end result is well worth the effort. There are tools to help you do the job and of course you can devise your own. Narrow-necked containers are easier to keep sealed. Corks, screw tops or just a piece of plastic fastened over the top with a rubber band all are satisfactory as covers. The container you select will be determined by where you plan to place it. Beverage bottles are fine, but there are many kinds and styles of terrariums made commercially that you can choose from; also, an old fish tank or glass pickle jar are all suitable. Use your imagination; you do not have to limit yourself to the commonplace.

Select and Restrain

Since terrariums are contained containers, you will have to be very careful about the kinds of plants you grow and restrain yourself as to quantity. Plants should all be slow growers, be small in scale, have similar habits, and be compatible. By compatibles I mean plants that will be happy growing together and not compete for space and light and all grow at about the same rate. By limiting yourself — depending on the size of container — to no more than three to five plants or better still only one, you can avoid the need to refurbish and/or replant every three or four months as is required for the heavily overplanted kinds you find offered commercially.

In essence, a multi-planted terrarium is a miniature landscape and should be designed as such. Therefore plants selected should have good contrast, form, texture, and color in addition to the aforementioned requirements. A simple collection could include a *Saxifraga stolonifera* "Strawberry geranium", a *Pteris multifida* "Table-fern," and a *Pilea repens* "Black leaf panamiga." If you stick to only one plant per container as I often have to do with narrow-necked wine bottles, you may not have to refurbish or replant for years. Any of the selaginellas are suitable for this kind of growing as well as the *Marchantia polymorpha* "Liverwort".

You can try any plant that will fit into the terrarium. Never limit yourself to the tried and true. You'd be amazed at what you can develop. There's no such word as can't when gardening indoors or out — it may take a bit of doing but in the majority of instances you can. For example the plantlet of *Episcia cuperata* 'Silver Sheen' that was started in a terrarium at the same time as I shifted the mother plant into a 3-inch pot is, in just three months, about twice the size of its parent. It may soon grow out of its wine bottle home but in the meantime look at all the fun I've had watching it grow on the east window sill just above my desk. Despite the air roots that have formed at each node (the axil of each leaf stem), the plant appears pleasing to the eye.

Basics for Planting a Terrarium

First things first — the day before you begin to plant, wash your container (new, old, etc.) thoroughly; rinse with clear, clean, cold water; and let it *drain dry* overnight. This pre-preparation prevents gravel, dust, and/or soil mix from clinging to the sides as you plant through the mouth of a narrow container. The same holds true for easy-access containers that have sparkling clean, dry insides. Use a funnel or a self-made paper cone for pouring the soil. It controls the matter into a steady narrow stream as it pours into the container, thereby saving a heavy cleaning job on the wall sides after everything is planted. It is always best to use the smallest size of a plant variety — specifically, rooted plants grown either in thumb pots up to those in 2- and 1½-inch pots.

Assemble the following materials: plants; gravel (parakeet, fish tank or washed river sand); a well-mixed growing medium that consists of by volume three parts commercially prepared, sterilized potting soil for house plants, three parts horticultural grade perlite and one part gravel or sand — I prefer to use parakeet gravel because of its texture and the charcoal and crushed shells that are added to it by most manufacturers; assorted tools, such as the long-handled ones illustrated or those of your own devising plus the funnel and a turkey baster and/or a mister — Windex bottles with spray tops are satisfactory if you don't have the other kinds offered in plant supply outlets.

Line the bottom with at least ½" of gravel. I like to hill it in such a way that there is ½" of gravel in the front rising slowly to about 1" at the back. Once you have achieved this or any other basic terrain that suits your pleasure, pour a ½" to 1" layer of soil mix over this, carefully following the contours of your mini-landscape. If the container is large enough, you may even consider terracing so that the plants will sit at different levels. With a plan in mind, gently push out pockets for your plants with a digging tool such as a small teaspoon or the long-handled terrarium spoon.

Wide-necked terrariums. If the mouth of the terrarium is wide enough for you to work your hand in, merely tap out the plants from their pots, gently shake off as much soil as you can, and trim the root ball so that it can be completely covered when planted without

Episcia cuperata 'Silver Sheen' after two months at an east window

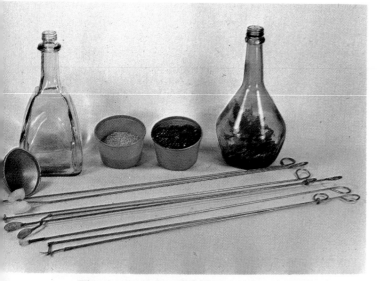

These materials will help you grow a terrarium. Back row, from left to right: sparkling clear and dry bottle; container with bird gravel; container filled with regular potting soil; green bottle terrarium containing a fern that has been growing in a west window. Front row: aluminum funnel; "Shovel Tool" to dry inside terrarium; "Bottle Sponge" to wipe wall; "Tamper Tool" to gently press soil down around plants; "Planter Tool" to insert plants through neck of bottle; "Leaf Duster" to remove debris from leaves and container; "Cutter Tool" to assist in cutting off and removing unwanted leaves. — Tools from A. & N. Terrarium Tool Co.

raising the existing soil level. With a teaspoon, fill in the open spaces around the roots with a bit of extra soil, and gently tamp it down in and around the plant without changing the contour of the landscape. At your discretion, decorate the mini-garden with a white sand river, a rock path, or single mini-boulder, some driftwood twigs and/or a figurine or two. All should be in scale and become part of the whole. Now mist down the side walls and the top of the soil until the gravel layer appears damp. Seal the top and set the terrarium into filtered light for a few days before bringing it out into full light. The plants need this time for adjustment, and recuperation from the transplant shock. Follow this practice for all transplants for best results.

Medium-wide-necked terrariums. If the mouth of your terrarium is too narrow for you to use your hands, yet considerably wider than the neck of a standard whiskey or wine bottle, dig out your plant pockets with a long-handled spoon. Then tap out each plant from its pot and rinse off at least ¾ of the soil clinging to the root ball — always use a gentle, tepid spray rather than a cold, forceful one. With sharp scissors, trim the roots back to about half their original size and pat damp dry the remaining roots and soil with absorbent paper towels. Now forming a tube, roll each plant tightly, without crushing, into a sheet of typing paper or loose leaf paper — any kind of paper will do as long as it doesn't deteriorate rapidly when moist. Slip the paper-rolled plant through the mouth opening and set it down into its assigned space. With long-handled tweezer or pincers, slip off the paper and lift it out of the container. With the tamper, gently press the soil down on and around the roots. Water down with a mister or a turkey baster by letting the water dribble down the sides of the glass and then seal the top. This method takes a bit of practice but it works.

Narrow-necked terrariums. For narrow-necked bottles, funnel sand and soil as suggested for the other methods. Prepare the holes for planting with a long-handled teaspoon or digger. Instead of using plants with full root systems, I find it easier to plant cuttings, offsets, plantlets, or tiny ferns that have just begun to show their first two true fronds. Tiny pteris ferns are ideally suited for narrow neck planting. For rooted cuttings, rinse off all the soil. Pick the plants up with a long-handled tweezer or plant gripper in such a way that you can slip the plant in through the mouth of the bottle without crushing any of the parts and stick it into its new growing place. If I'm lucky, I make a direct hit into the plant hole and can release and plant immediately. Otherwise, I pull out the gripping tool and replace it with a long stick or digging tool and work the plant into its hole. After it is set, I tamp down the soil as best I can around the roots, water down the soil with the turkey baster, seal the top and set aside until ready to place in its permanent home.

Terrarium-grown plants require a minimum of care and water/fertilizing; just an occasional removal of a browned off leaf or, if something goes wrong, total replacement of a plant that won't or can't adapt.

Depending on the size of plants and container, you may not have to add water more often than once every three months; some, when properly cared for, no more often than once a year!!! Use your gravel base color as your guide. It will lighten when watering is required. Water with a very light hand via the mister or turkey baster system. Often a mere teaspoonful of water will suffice and rarely more than half a cup. If you just happen to over water and find water sloshing around at the soil level *Do Not* pour it out. Everything in the planter will pour out with it. Remove the excess water as you can by siphoning off with a long straw or if the mouth of the container is wide enough, slurp it up with the turkey baster. Also, keep the cover off the top of the mouth to permit rapid evaporation of any inaccessible moisture. When you observe that the glisten has disappeared from the top soil layer you can reseal and grow on as before. Too much water can cause root rot and too little, wilt and browning off. Water by eyedropper rather than by cup.

It may take a while to attain a finished product when you "sparse" plant but it is by far more gratifying than the "instant" planted commercial offerings.

The terrarium on the left contains Marchantia polymorpha *"Liverwort". The terrarium on the right also contains a "Liverwort" that didn't make it, due to overwatering. These plants enjoy a very high humidity but not wet swamp-like conditions.*

Both wine bottles contain two frond fern starts that have developed into good small plants. Note the different bottle tops.

Selaginella krausiana denticulata *"Trailing Irish moss" is good for covered terrarium culture. However, it does require an occasional (once a week) lift off of cover to perform best.*

Recycled wine bottles. The green bottle contains young plants of Kalanchoe pinnata *"Air plant," the clear one* Episcia *cuperata 'Silver Sheen'.*

Greenhouses

Free-standing greenhouse

There is a greenhouse for most every situation from the simple, unheated lean-to made up from a lathe frame covered with heavy duty plastic to a totally automated thermopane free-standing house installed on a city apartment house rooftop that looks out over the Manhattan skyline. A unit can cost as little as $50.00 or as much as you want to spend. Before making any decisions consider some of the following questions. How much time do you devote to your hobby? What kinds of plants do you plan to grow and how many? What kind of site do you plan to place it on, taking into consideration that it should be placed so that it gets the most available light possible during the shortest darkest days of winter. A site location on the south or southeast side of the house is best and in descending order southwest, west and north. Partial shade is desirable in the summer as offered from the house shadow or from trees and shrubs. However, it is important to consider the possibility of damage to the greenhouse from falling branches.

The best site for your greenhouse is one that is nearly level and drains well with full exposure to the south. If it slopes, it should slope slightly to the south which, as every good farmer and gardener knows, is the best kind of siting for growing crops and gardens. Also a preferred must is to have or provide a wind break of trees on the side of the prevailing winds such as those one observes on the north and west sides of mid-west prairie farms.

What size and style will you require to best meet your requirements? If you plan to build it yourself (pre-fab or from scratch), how handy are you with tools? Do you want to have it fully automated (heat, ventilation, supplemental lighting, misting, etc.)? What will the costs be for heating and cabling in your locale? Do you want to include a slop sink and potting bench or can you do without? How available and close is your water supply? Piping water can become an expensive proposition. I could go on and on from decisions about the kinds of benches and floors to ideas about automated watering systems and so forth. My best suggestion is to contact your local county agent. He/she can advise you about what size and set-up is probably best for you; what local building codes and zoning

*Penthouse roof garden
overlooking the Empire State Building
in New York City*

laws are applicable; and give you the names of people in your area who have their own greenhouses with whom you can consult about the dos and don'ts of building a greenhouse. Also, these people will make an excellent source for cuttings and rooted plants as well as a fount of information about the what, where, when and how to of plants and supplies. For best results plan on growing plants that all have about the same temperature and humidity requirements. Adjusting for light is a simple matter; shade lovers can be placed under benches or in corners; moderate light plants on the benches; and all others on benches or glass

Multi-crop greenhouse

*Arched greenhouse filled
with blooming plants
arranged to take best advantage
of the light*

Lean-to greenhouse

shelves attached to the sides of the greenhouse or individually hung from hooks or chains inserted into the center ridge of the greenhouse.

For most efficient use of space and energy, grow plants that will require little or no auxiliary heating or cooling. Some plants that meet this criteria are the 3,000 plus varieties of Geraniums and Pelargoniums as well as the multitudes of cacti and succulents. If grown dry, most of these plants will survive winter night temperatures that go as low as 25°F+ and summer temperatures that often climb to as high as 110°F+ when you will probably have to water the plants at least

twice a day to keep them from cooking and collapsing. I know that plants will survive through these extremes in temperature because I've observed and have been involved in both situations. My friend — the one who can grow those beautiful maple bonsais — grows all the plants in his cactus and succulent house as follows. Starting in September, he begins to withhold water from the plants by watering thoroughly only when the soil is bone dry. By mid-November he merely gives the plants and soil a light sprinkling of water. Thereafter and on until the beginning of March he withholds moisture completely. He will look into the house

41

Interior view of built-out window sill greenhouse

An eclectic collection of greenhouse-grown plants being summered outdoors.

perhaps once every two weeks during this dry period to check for and remove plants that don't make it due to various reasons such as pest infestation and of course the cold. I know of instances where the outside temperature has dropped as low as 10°F during midwinter, yet without even a space heater to bring the temperature up a bit most of his plants came through.

My own experience involves an extremely high heat situation that I encountered a number of years ago while working on a selection job in an East coast greenhouse during a summer heat wave. The project I was concerned with was to learn the cause of and then control and eradication of "Crook Neck" in commercial bedding geranium varieties such as the then very popular 'Olympic Red'. Working on this project in 110°-120°F temperatures was not easy by any means. However, I am still here among the living, and the descendents from the line of plants that I selected out and propagated are still around to enhance many a garden bed and planter.

There is no limit to the kinds of plants you can grow in a green house as long as you can provide them with the amount of temperature and humidity that they require. Light — the most essential factor for plant growth and maintenance and the most difficult to provide in most interior situations — is the one condition that you will not have to concern yourself about providing for most plants and crops. In fact you may have to consider "shading" all or part of the "glass" during the summer when your ventilating and cooling systems are unable to compensate for extreme heat buildup and the sun's rays are so strong that it burns through and often destroys flower, foliage or the entire plant. This is why you will find many a greenhouse grower either heavily shading his "glass" or emptying his benches and summering his plants outdoors.

The difference between window sill and greenhouse growing is that in a greenhouse light is available to your plants from at least three directions (top, side, and front) whereas on a window sill they are only exposed to front window light. There are a number of ways for you to obtain three dimensional light even if your lot is too small to support a greenhouse or even if there is no way to install a lean to. If you are building a new home, have your architect design a room that includes a greenhouse-type wall. Or, if you have plans to alter or update an older house, the greenhouse window/wall could also be considered for inclusion if you are into plants in more than a casual way. Of late, hobby greenhousers have become so numerous that as with other plant specialties, they too have formed a society for the exchange of ideas, information, and friendly communications. For further information about this national group contact:

Mrs. W.O. Mall
The Hobby Greenhouse Owners Association of America
18 Echo
Corte Madera, California 94925

Work bench
with soil bin

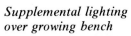

Supplemental lighting
over growing bench

Venting
a greenhouse

Add-on deck
greenhouse

Summer flowers in winter snow

Outside view of arched add-on greenhouse

Top Performers

These are a group of plants (some new and some that were originally special interest hobby plants) that are widely distributed top performers that are now available to the public since the publication of *Houseplants and Indoor Landscaping.* I have observed and grown them for at least three years and feel at this time that I can give you some solid practical advice about their care and culture.

For convenience sake all plants will be in alphabetical order according to their botanical name; their common name(s) will follow in quotation marks.

Light requirements will be indicated as follows:

Low light — sites that offer from 25-100 foot candles

Medium light — sites that offer from 100-1,000 foot candles

Full light — sites that are usually located in front of a south or west window, in a greenhouse, or at the center parts of fluorescent tubes when grown under artificial light.

Adromischus maculatus
"Calico hearts"

Full light to medium — this stonecrop is a low, slow growing succulent that performs well in a greenhouse, on a window sill or even at the ends of a fluorescent lamp. Water/fertilize only when the dipstick is completely dry. This plant, given sufficient light intensity, will produce red-white tipped flowers.

Aeonium archrichsym

Full to medium light — a charming shrub-like slow-growing succulent that prefers to have its

Adromischus maculatus
"Calico hearts"

soil quite moist yet thoroughly drained. This is the only way I've found to prevent heavy leaf drop. An excellent pot plant, its character and growing habit also lends itself to the bonsai style. You can grow the plant in the greenhouse, on the window sill or in the light garden.

Aloe variegata ausana
"Partridge-breast"

This is one plant that you'll be able to hand down to your grandchildren. Almost indestructible, it prefers a well-drained soil that completely dries out between each water/fertilizing. It prefers a medium to full light situation and will adapt quite well to the light available at the ends of a fluorescent tube. A slow grower, it does have a tendency to lean to light. This should be kept under control by giving it a half turn about once a week or you will soon find it leaning out of its pot. This is a fine plant for greenhouse, sill, light garden, or even a site no more than five feet in from a window.

Aloe aristata
"Lace aloe"

My all time favorite. When grown properly, it is sure to win a blue ribbon in a flower show because of its interesting leaf form and regular growing habit. A full light plant, it prefers a west window and makes an excellent greenhouse subject as well as light garden plant when grown under the center part of the lamps. For best effect grow it as round as you can in an Azalea pot (it's flatter) rather than the standard form pots. Set in the center of the pot, the leaves should extend over the lip and the entire plant should form a lacy rosette. It prefers an evenly damp, well-drained soil and should only be thoroughly water/fertilized when the dip stick is moist one half the way up from the bottom.

Aeonium archrichsym
grown as a bonsai

grown as a pot plant

Aloe variegata ausana
"Partridge breast"

Aloe aristata
"Lace aloe"

BEGONIAS

Rieger begonias

Recently introduced to the trade and public, Rieger begonias have been welcomed by all who see these heavy-blooming, constantly-flowering, flamboyant plants. The Aphrodite strain is trailing in habit and has mostly semi-double to double flowers with a good color range in pink, rose, and red. The Schwabenland kinds are more upright in growth and have single to semi-double flowers. These have a color range of white, yellow, vibrant reds, orange, rose and pink. Best grown in 5- to 6-inch pots, they will not require transplanting for at least a year. All prefer a full light situation such as in a greenhouse, in an east or west window, or weather permitting, outdoors. Water/fertilize only when the dip stick is moist about one half the way up from the bottom. Although grown in exactly the same exposure and in exactly the same growing medium, I have observed that the Schwabenland kinds require less frequent watering. The reason I do not suggest them for the light garden is because they do take up a lot of space by spreading out and reaching up into the tubes. These plants will require more grooming than most because of their prolific blooms and resultant florette drop. You will also find that some of the foliage will have to be removed when it begins to brown/dry off and drops on the soil. However these little chores should not deter you from growing these beauties. Do not be in a rush to remove the flowering panicles. Some will produce as many as twenty florets while others will form leaves and branches that will continue to grow on as part of the plant.

Begonia semperflorens albo-foliis
"Calla lily begonia"

This pink-flowering, ever-blooming, white to white and green foliaged plant prefers full to moderate light such as that found in a greenhouse or in the center of a

Schwabenland Red

light garden. Its growing medium should be well drained yet constantly damp. It will perform on a west or east window sill if you can find a way of providing at least a 50% humidity around it and adequate air circulation. Water/fertilize when the top of the soil feels dry, making sure that the excess water drains out of the soil and that the plant does not stand on wet feet. Pick off and discard all discolored foliage and flowers. This is essential for the health of the plant and to avoid invasion of fungus diseases.

Begonia
'Beatrice Haddrell'

This small, slow-growing, showy plant will perform well in most any interior site that receives at least an intensity of light strong enough to read in. The lower the light value, the larger and paler the foliage will be. The stronger the light value, the tighter the growth will be with intense deep chocolate-brown, very hairy foliage. Keep them away from windows that will expose them to strong sunlight because it will burn the leaves and produce round burn out patches. The longer you put off repotting, the slower the plant will grow. Of course, there comes a time in the life of every plant when it must be repotted but for space sake as well as a growth retardant, hold off as long as possible. Water/fertilize thoroughly whenever the dipstick measures moist one half the way up from the bottom. Groom and clean as you would the other begonias.

Improved Schwabenland Pink

Begonia semperflorens albo-foliis
"Calla lily begonia"

Schwabenland Twinkles

Begonia 'Beatrice Haddrell'
Two-inch thumb pot

Begonia 'Beatrice Haddrell'
Two 3-inch pots six months later. Left are grown at the end of a tube in the nursery shelf; right are in the center of the same shelf.

Begonia
Amy

A curiosity that you may encounter during your travels and in private collections. The habit of some Rex begonias commonly known as "Painted Leaf" or "Fan" begonias to produce plantlets at the point of union of the principal veins of a leaf is not uncommon. This method of plant increase was reported as long ago as 1868 in Belgique Horticole by Charles Chevalier. I have known 'Amy' as a greenhouse subject but I am quite sure, given the space, it will perform quite well in the confines of a high humidity artificial light garden. Water/fertilize when the dipstick reads moist one half up from the bottom. To better maintain the mother plant, it is suggested that all leaves that manifest the piggy back growing habit be removed. If you wish to increase your plants by rooting a plantlet, set it into a small pot filled with moistened growing medium by pinning the leaf down into the soil. Keep it attached to the mother plant until it forms roots and then clip it off to grow on its own.

Begonia 'Amy'

Begonia 'Amy'

Begonia rex
Fairy

From my experience, a slow growing compact plant that is most suitable for the light garden where its delicate silvery pink-hued leaves serve as a foil for the thicker angular types of plants that it is grown with in a compatible garden. This is also excellent as a greenhouse plant or as a sill subject where you can maintain a high humidity. (See *Houseplants and Indoor Landscaping.*) It will perform best in moderate to full light as long as it is diffused. Water/fertilize when dipstick is moist one half up from the bottom.

Begonia rex 'Fairy'

Billbergia nutans
"Queen's tears" or "Indoor oats"

An easy-to-care-for interior plant, it will adapt and perform satisfactorily in most any situation where the light is strong enough for you to read by. Because of its size and growing habit, it also makes a fine plant for the light garden. Its flower stalk carries pink bracts with green flowers edged with blue violet. The stem and flowers retain their color and form for many months even after it has ceased blooming and dried. You can increase the plant by removing and planting up the rooted off-shoots. Since this is an epiphyte that has adapted to pot plant culture, you will find that it is essential when watering to keep the center urn of leaves filled with water at all times and to water/fertilize the soil whenever the dipstick is moist one half way up from the bottom.

Billbergia nutans
"Queen's tears" or "Indoor oats"

Cryptanthus bivittatus minor
"Dwarf rose striped star" (roseus pictus).

A native of Brazil, this plant is found growing on rocks and on the forest floor. Small in size and slow growing in habit it is ideal for the dish garden, terrarium, light garden and as a small table plant. A moderate light plant, it will adapt to poor light as well as the kind of light available in an unobstructed east window. It can be propagated from offsets and should be thoroughly water/fertilized when the soil/growing medium is dry to touch.

To find out more about the "Bromeliads" and about their forms, colors, and situation suitability, see *Houseplants and Indoor Landscaping*.

Cryptanthus bivittatus minor
"Dwarf rose striped star"

Aporocactus flagelliformis
"Rat tail cactus"

Chamaecerus silvestre
"Peanut cactus"

Cephalocereus senilis
"Old man cactus"

Schlumbergera bridgessi
"Christmas cactus"

Both plants were started at the same time and grown under exactly the same conditions. Yet one is larger and faster-growing than the other. These plants are approximately two years old. Both are grown in the light garden during the short days of winter and then moved to a west window from April through October.

Year-old cactus seedlings that have just been planted up into their first growing pots. These are kept in the light garden nursery shelf all together in the drawer organizer and will only be shifted up to the next size pot when they begin to touch each other. These plants, all different, were germinated from a packet of seeds.

CACTACEAE OR CACTUS

Members of *Cactaceae* are about the easiest to grow and maintain in almost every interior situation. Most will put on a riotous show of color at least once a year. Some will bloom in their first year while others may take as long as fifty or more years. Some have massive showy flowers; others may require the services of a magnifying glass.

Varied in habit, form and flower, cacti can be found growing in most arid regions of the western hemisphere from the Arctic Circle on south to Patagonia on the southern tip of South America.

Many of the "Jungle cactus" such as *Schlumbergera bridgessi* "Christmas cactus" are found growing in the trees of a tropical rain forest. These plants can be recognized by their flattened, leaf-like, waxy green, glossy joints.

Most cacti are easily recognized by their needles and cushion-like areoles on the surface of the plant which serve the same function as the internodes (spaces between the joints) in other plants and from which all growth occurs such as flowers, spines, bristles and branches.

An ideal group of plants for the cool greenhouse, many of these will also adapt to interior situations where the light intensity is as little as fifty foot candles; and, during their regular growing season, they often will tolerate average night temperatures as low as 45°F. Of course, the more light and heat the needled kinds are exposed to the more prolific their bloom and the more vigorous their growth.

Since no two varieties have the same requirements, I suggest that those grown in an average interior situation other than a greenhouse be water/fertilized thoroughly at least two days after the growing medium is bone dry. Depending on where you grow your plants, you may have to water/fertilize as often as every third day during the summer months and perhaps no more than once a month when the winter days are shortest.

Cactus can be propagated from cuttings or parts broken off at the nodes (joints). Pot these up as soon as they are taken and grow them on as you would the parent plant. Growing them from seed will take a bit longer to produce a 4-inch sized pot plant, but it can be a fun project to try. For best results follow the directions on the seed packet. Seed can be obtained via mail order or sometimes can be found among the seed packets of a general display.

Orchid cactus species

Mammillaria sartorii

Echinocereus cinerascens

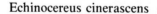

Mammillaria woodsii

Orchid cactus species
(Probably rosetta)

Gymnocalycium denudatum

Ariocarpus kotschubeyanus

Gymnocalycium damsii

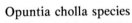
Opuntia cholla species

Gymnocalycium friedrickii

Echinocereus reichenbachii

Astrophytum capricorne

Stenocactus species

Parodia sanguiniflora

Mammillaria zeilmanniana

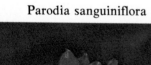

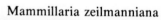

Gymnocalycium bruchii

Cephalocereus palmerii

Neoporteria nigrihorrida

Mammillaria spinossissima

Astrophytum myriostigma

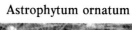

Notocactus graessneri

Astrophytum ornatum

55

Opuntia rufida

Monvillea spegazzinii

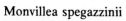

Echinocereus triglochidatus

Gymnocalycium baldianum

Ferocactus latispinus

Malacocarpus erinacea

56

Opuntia acicularis

Gymnocalycium denudatum

Leuchtenbergia principis

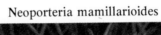

Neoporteria mamillarioides

Notocactus haselbergii

Notocactus caespitosus

Chamaecereus silvestrii

Notocactus scopa

Astrophytum myriostigma

Mammillaria prolifera

Notocactus tabularis

Martimacereus nanus

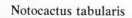

Opuntia species

Astrophytum asterias

Mammillaria bocasana

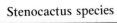

Stenocactus species

Opuntia vestita

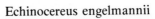

Echinocereus engelmannii

Dolichothele sphaerica

Opuntia acicularis

Ariocarpus kotschubeyanus

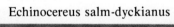

Echinocereus pentalophus

Ferocactus latispinus

Echinocereus salm-dyckianus

Ceropegia woodii
"Rosary vine" or "String of hearts"

These charming plants are suitable for hanging baskets and can be grown in most interior situations where the light intensity is at least strong enough to read by. Mine is grown near the end of the tubes in a light garden. I have also had satisfactory results with this variety grown in a west window. The plant produces small violet to purple lantern-like flowers which mature into tubers that will produce new plants if set onto some growing medium. You can do this to either increase your plant population or, as I have, to form a mat of foliage and flower that covers the soil in the pot. It was only after this mat was formed that I permitted the plant to trail over the rim. A comparatively slow grower, it took my one original plant about a year to produce enough growth to cover over the soil in a 6-inch pot. Water/fertilize when dipstick measures damp two thirds up from the bottom.

Chamaecyparis obtusa nana
"Dwarf hinokicypress"

This dwarf form of its much larger growing relative is perfect for container culture since it rarely grows taller or wider than two feet. A full light plant, it will adapt to interior situations where the light is no less than 55 foot candles. You may grow it on in a pot or consider it is an eventual subject for bonsai. In any event, I will continue to grow my plant and train it in its growing pot until it has put on sufficient growth and becomes root bound. Then, I can prune it out to show the wood and trim the foliage so that it will all be in scale and give the appearance of a miniature tree. Only at this time will I either repot the plant back into its original pot by removing as much of the soil as possible from the roots as well as pruning them back to one third of their original length and width; or, following the same root-prune, soil-removal procedure, plant it into a Japanese-style bonsai container with perhaps some pebbles to indicate a path or water and/or a rock to indicate a mountain that will give scale to the tree and landscape. (See *Punica granatum* for the aforementioned procedure.) Right now my plant is enjoying its nursery setting at the center of the tubes in the light garden. It has adapted to a once weekly watering. If you grow it on a sill or in a greenhouse, water/fertilize when the dipstick measures moist one half way up from the bottom.

Ceropegia woodii
"Rosary vine" or "String of hearts"

Chamaecyparis obtusanana
"Dwarf hinokicypress"

Coleus grown under fluorescent "grow" lamp

Coleus

Although coleus have been illustrated and discussed in *Houseplants and Indoor Landscaping,* I felt that you should see the intensity of color that develops and compactness of growth that can be attained when grown under a fluorescent "grow" lamp. Also coleus — in all their vibrant color and forms — make excellent plants for practically every interior situation. For the inexperienced interior gardener they will often serve as a guide as to when to water or when not to. You can root pieces in water and watch them develop roots. And, since they are about the least expensive houseplant you can find, you will feel free to experiment with them and be able to learn on your own how to be a more observant gardener. You may even try to grow enough cuttings so that you can set them out into your garden or plant them in patio tubs.

Coleus Carefree Jade and Carefree Scarlet in Jiffy-Tubs

Crassula pseudolycopodioides
"Princess pine"

This small, slow-growing succulent will perform best in moderate light. Its sprawling habit makes it an excellent small basket subject as well as an ideal table plant within a room. It is also fine for end-of-tube growing as well as for sill and greenhouse culture. It rarely needs repotting and can be kept in bounds by trimming off excess growth. The trimmings will root quite rapidly if you stick the ends at least one quarter of an inch down into the growing medium. Succulent in nature, these plants will require a thorough water/fertilizing only when the dipstick is moist one fourth the way up from the bottom.

Cuphea hyssopifolia
"False heather"

A full light plant that blooms prolifically in a warm, high humidity situation, such as a greenhouse, or in a light garden when set directly under the center part of the tubes. This plant is a bit too fast a grower to meet my requirements because, even when grown in a 5-inch pot, it outgrew its assigned light garden space within three months. It also required an almost daily water/fertilizing to keep the foliage from curling and drying up. I do believe it would make a better greenhouse subject than to grow it in a regular interior space.

Cyperus alternifolius
"Umbrella plant"

This bog plant has adapted to artificial light culture at the end of the tubes as well as to the once a week water/fertilizing program. A moderate light plant, it will perform quite well in the lower reading light situations. A comparatively slow grower as you can see from the pictures, one taken in February and the other in June of the same year, it appears quite content with its placement on the floor driftwood

Cuphea hyssopifolia
"False heather"

Crassula pseudolycopodioides
"Princess pine"

Cyperus alternifolius
"Umbrella plant"
In June

Cyperus alternifolius
"Umbrella plant"
In February

light garden. It does produce a rampant root system that will grow out from the bottom of the pot to reach out in all directions. This can be controlled in one of two ways. Give the plant a half turn each time it is watered or, if this doesn't work, just cut off the roots as they reach out from the bottom of the pot. If you like to arrange flowers, you'll find that a few stems used

for your line or the heads used as filler or accent are always there when you want them. Also, you can cut and dry some for use in dried arrangements. The easiest method I know of to increase these plants is to pot up the stolons (plantlets) as they form (see illustrations) and cut them away from the mother plant after they have formed sufficient roots to grow on their own.

Davallia fejeensis plumosa
"Dainty rabbit's-foot"

Davallia fejeensis plumosa
"Dainty rabbit's-foot"

I thought you might like to know how I was able to start this plant. I was given a cluster of furry rhizomes to grow for a friend who was having some difficulty maintaining her mother plant. Since this was my first propagating encounter with this kind of plant, I decided that it best not be planted directly into the soil but should have some contact with it. Instead of using the usual hair pin method to fasten down this ungainly "Rabbit's-foot," I resorted to a handy rubber band. The plant was then placed atop a piece of driftwood close up to the center of the light garden about six inches from the lights. There it sat for approximately three months with no sign of life other than a touch of green at the tips of its paws. It wasn't until the fourth month that it began to show signs of growth and, after producing its sixth frond, it popped its rubber band. This is a full light plant that requires a higher humidity and temperature than that found in the average home or office. Therefore for best growing results, I suggest that it be grown either in a light garden or a greenhouse. I do know of davallias that have adapted to interior space growing but the need for a daily dip to keep the moss-covered growing basket moist to create a high humidity micro-climate really wasn't worth the effort.

Dizygotheca elegantissima
"Spider aralia"
Grown under lights and being trained as a bonsai.

Dizygotheca elegantissima
"Spider aralia"
Grown under natural light

Dizygotheca elegantissima
"Spider aralia"

A plant for most interior spaces where there is full light, it will adapt to situations no further than five feet from natural window light. Best of all, it can be dwarfed and trained into a feathery delicate Bonsai and maintained in the light garden. Note how much darker and thicker the foliage is when grown under lights in comparison to a window floor plant grown in the natural light of an eastern exposure. Water when dipstick reads moist one half way up from the bottom.

Echeveria multicaulis
"Copper rose"

Ideal for west window culture or in the greenhouse, it will also adapt to table culture no further than five feet from a natural light source. Under optimum full light conditions, it can be brought into bloom when the daylength is twelve hours or longer. It will continue to do so until the days begin to shorten to less than twelve hours.

Because of its succulent nature, it is best for single pot culture where it can be watered only two days after the dipstick indicates bone dry rather than in a mixed collection such as a light garden or plantscape where a high humidity situation may cause it to rot rather than grow.

Episcia dianthiflora
"Lace flower vine"

The plant in the white pot was pictured in my first book *Houseplants and Indoor Landscaping;* now three years later the same plant has developed from a single tiny plant growing in a thumb pot to a massive mat that has begun to overflow its 8-inch pot borders. I still haven't gotten it to produce the white carnation-like blooms for which it is named. I do believe that if I had kept it pot bound by limiting it to a 5-inch growing pot, it would have bloomed at least a year ago. Its tiny green velvet leaves are most pleasing to look at and more than compensate for its lack of bloom. A medium light plant, it is suitable for most interior situations where it can be exposed to natural or artificial light for a minimum of

Episcia dianthiflora
"Lace flower vine"

Episcia dianthiflora
"Lace flower vine"
Three years later

ten hours a day. It does prefer a higher humidity than is usually found in a home situation, but it will adapt to sill culture. I've grown this plant as a hanging basket in an east window and then in the light garden when our November days shortened to eight hours and less. When grown alone, water/fertilize when the dipstick reads moist two thirds up from the bottom.

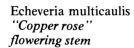

Echeveria multicaulis
"Copper rose"
flowering stem

Echeveria multicaulis
"Copper rose"

Episcia cuperata
'Silver sheen'

Eucalyptus globulus
"Blue gum"

Episcia cuperata
'Silver sheen'
Set up close to
the lights

Episcia cuperata
Silver Sheen

A medium light plant, it prefers a constantly damp soil that is thoroughly drained. Kept pot bound, it will bloom constantly. The daily water/fertilizing that is required to keep it at its peak of growth and performance is well worth the effort. Because of its spreading growing habit, it will make a suit-able- hanging plant for greenhouse culture or can be grown as a trailing plant in the light garden. For more information, see the chapter "Artificial Light Gardening."

Eucalyptus globulus
"Blue gum"

The seed of this plant was a bonus from the pods and branches I collected one winter near San Simeon in California, to use for some dried arrangements. The seed fell from the pods on the kitchen table as I was cleaning up the branches and preparing them for storage until I needed them for our local spring flower show. Never one to waste even a seed, I swept up all that I could find into an envelope for future distribution to garden club members. The two remaining seeds that I missed in the first sweep up were planted in a thumb pot and set into the nursery shelf. One seed germinated in three days while the other I'll have to presume lost. Although the main stem was very weak, and all the lower leaves soon browned off each time it put forth two new top leaves, the plant persisted in its effort to live and grow. After growing like this for about two months, I decided to give it more growing room and shifted it up into a 3-inch pot. This move checked its growth for at least a month, but I am now pleased to report that it has started to take off in all directions and may soon match the vigor of its outdoor-grown relatives. This plant has a-dapted quite well to light garden culture and, if it continues as it has, it will soon become a bonsai candidate. The typical aromatic Eucalyptus fragrance was recognizable from the onset of its first two leaves and will add interest wherever it is grown.

Eucalyptus globulus
"Blue gum"
Mature tree
grown outdoors

Eugenia myrtifolia
"Australian bush cherry"

Eugenia myrtifolia
"Australian bush cherry"

A full light plant formerly relegated to the greenhouse, it has adapted beautifully to sill as well as light garden culture. This shrub lends itself to training and pruning and is often grown indoors and outdoors (climate permitting) as a topiary. Now a bit tall for my light garden, it will eventually be cut back, pruned out and planted in a bonsai pot. It will then be placed in the light garden with my other dwarfed tropical tree and shrub specimens. At present it appears to be quite content to grow, form buds, and flower on a west window sill where passers-by knock on my door to ask about it.

This plant is on a demand water/fertilizing program since it does have a tendency to drop leaves and flower buds if the soil is permitted to dry out too much. Water thoroughly every time the dipstick is moist two thirds up from the bottom. This plant will let you know soon enough about when to water by dropping a leaf or two.

Euphorbia mammillaris
"Corn cob cactus"

Euphorbia obesa
"Turkish temple" or "Baseball plant"

Euphorbia mammillaris
"Corn cob cactus"

A native of the Cape Province in South Africa, this Eastern Hemisphere "spurge" is not a cactus but is an example of the kind of succulent that developed in arid regions of the Eastern Hemisphere while the cactus developed in the West. This "conversation piece" succulent with its spines and corncob aspect may be grown in any interior living space where there is at least medium light. Water/fertilize at least two days after its dipstick is totally dry.

Euphorbia obesa
"Turkish temple" or "Baseball plant"

Rarely growing larger than five inches, this plant prefers a temperature of at least 62°F and medium light of at least 500 foot candles. Mine are grown on a west window. The female plant is globular in form while the male plant is rather pear shaped. Since these plants can be propagated only from seed, it is important that you protect the seeds from shooting out when they are mature by lightly covering the seed capsules with a bit of net. These plants are also South African natives, but I obtained mine at a local nursery. Water/fertilize two days after the dipstick is totally dry.

Euphorbia pulcherrima 'Ecke's White'
"White poinsettia"

A cultivar that has evolved from its Mexican ancestor via a breeding program instituted by Paul Ecke of California, this plant prefers a growing temperature of at least 62°F and the kind of humidity available in a greenhouse situation. It will adapt to interior living areas and I have seen prime specimens growing as a living room floor plant near a floor to ceiling glassed picture window that faces east. These plants were greenhouse grown and placed in the aforementioned situation around Christmas. In order to keep the plants blooming and in presentable condition (they were magnificent), the temperature in the room averaged no more than 65°F. Soil was water/fertilized when the dipstick read moist one half way up from the bottom. It was not until after Easter that they showed some signs of deterioration and had to be relegated to a holding room until weather and night temperatures of at least 50° warranted planting them outdoors in their pots. In the fall, when the days shortened to less than twelve hours, they were lifted pot and all out of the ground and brought back into the naturally lighted 60°-65°F holding room until they began to show color in the bracts (the leaf-like parts that many think of as the flower). A holding room can be any interior space that has sufficient light (natural or otherwise), temperature, and humidity to maintain and grow plants that you may not wish to display. Pruning of the plants (if they require shaping or control of size) is best done just prior to setting them outside for summer growing. For the apartment dweller, who has no outdoor garden or extra room space, you can carry your plant(s) on the window sill where it will not be exposed to any light other than the natural kind. All poinsettias are short day plants which means that they will only bloom after the day shortens to twelve or less hours. Any added light such as just turning on a light for a few minutes at night will retard or stop budset.

Euphorbia pulcherrima *'Ecke's White'*
"White Poinsettia"

Ficus pumila
"Climbing fig" or Creeping fig"

Ficus benjamina
"Weeping fig"

Ficus benjamina
"Weeping fig"

This plant will adapt to light as low as 50 foot candles (low light) and air conditioned interior spaces. However it prefers to be grown where it is exposed to at least medium light and a temperature of at least 65°F. The 5-inch potted plant illustrated is now about eighteen inches tall and has been growing in the same pot on a west window for at least a year. This plant too is a candidate for my indoor bonsai collection and will be trained, pruned and replanted when the woody trunk thickens a bit more and takes on the appearance of greater age. In the meantime it will continue to grow in the same pot in order to restrain its root growth which is an adjunct to the dwarfing process. Water/fertilize thoroughly when the dipstick measures moist three quarters up from the bottom.

Ficus pumila (also known in horticulture as Ficus repens)
"Climbing fig" or "Creeping fig"

A tough, rampant grower, it will tolerate most interiors that have medium light of at least 100 foot candles. A little less than a year old, my plant has trailing stems that measure from three- to three-and-one-half feet long and occupies most of a west window in my kitchen. Heat sensitive, it will actually feel as if it is clinging to me when I brush by it. On an on demand watering schedule that is dependent on the kind of light and room temperature, it may require watering as often as every other day yet will go for a week at times before indicating it needs water by yellowing a few leaves and also dropping a few. I make it a practice to feel the soil each morning when I go into the kitchen. If the top soil feels dry to touch, I give it sixteen ounces of water/fertilizer. It's growing in an 8-inch pot with a self-reservoir saucer attached yet there never is a drop of spill from the saucer!!! About once every two weeks, I bring the plant to the sink and water it straight from the faucet until the water runs over and out of the saucer. When this stops, I place it back in the window. I'll

Gasteria x 'Hybrida'
"Oxtongue" or "Bowtie-plants"

Ginkgo biloba
"Maidenhair tree"

admit that this is more work and attention than I like, but it is so rewarding.

You need not grow it only as a hanging plant. Because of its woody stems, it can be trained as a bonsai and, working with the younger green growth, you can tie it to a wire, wood, or plastic form to form interesting topiary. Its natural "hold fasts" (like ivy roots that attach themselves to everything) make growing a topiary an easy, attractive project for display indoors.

Gasteria x 'Hybrida'
"Oxtongue" or "Bowtie-plants"

One of the least demanding of all the plants I know and grow. It is tolerant of most interior atmospheres and will adapt to low light situations and performs quite well where night temperatures are allowed to go as low as 50°F. Grown dry, they probably will survive the winter months in a cold greenhouse. Mine is grown at the end of the tubes of the light garden and serves as a foil for the feathery foliaged plants that it is grown with

in the second shelf rock garden. Other than an initial thorough water/fertilizing at the time it was placed in the garden, it has not been watered for at least six months. It relies on the high humidity micro-climate of the light garden and any excess water run off that may accumulate within the pebble bed after each weekly watering session. Handle this plant with care. Its sword like cutting leaf edge developed for its self-preservation will wound you at the touch. You can increase your plants by breaking out the offsets as they form and planting them up.

Ginkgo biloba
"Maidenhair tree"

Started in the light garden from collected seed, this plant, now one year old, has never had to contend with its natural outdoor growing conditions. Hopefully, it will not go dormant (lose its leaves in winter) and, when it has developed sufficiently to give the appearance of a full grown tree without growing much taller than its present six in-

ches, I plan of course to train it as an indoor bonsai. I'm quite sure that these plants will make good cool greenhouse subjects since I've seen some larger three- to four-year old plants that have adapted to this kind of culture. Due to lack of supplemental light to extend the daylength in the greenhouse to at least ten hours, these plants have gone dormant each winter.

If you are a sill gardener, you may be able to start a plant or two by gathering the seed in the fall and planting each in its own pot (the seed is as large as a hickory nut). Place each pot in its own plastic bag, twist tie the top to maintain a constant, high humidity and set it on your warmest, brightest window sill. Only open the plastic bag when the first two leaves appear. This can take anywhere from three to six months. Thereafter, grow it on as you would any full light loving young plant.

Haworthia cuspidata
"Star window plant"
in bloom

Hatiora salicornioides
"Drunkards dream"
A two-year-old plant grown for one year on an east
window sill and then transferred to the light
garden one pot in front of the tube ends

Haworthia cuspidata
"Star window plant"
With offsets

Hatiora salicornioides
"Drunkards dream"

A full light plant that will adapt to medium light. An excellent subject for tables, sills, light gardens and in the greenhouse. Very slow growing in habit, it may not have to be shifted to a larger growing pot no more often than every two to three years. Normally spreading in habit, it can be developed into a small hanging basket plant. Although it will take a lot of abuse, it does tend to drop some of its bottle shaped branches if handled roughly. Just stick one end into the pot soil and it will root to start a new plant. True to its succulent nature, it will only require a thorough water/fertilizing after the dipstick has been dry for at least two days.

Haworthia cuspidata
"Star window plant"

Another easy to grow succulent from South Africa that adapts to

Hatiora salicornioides
"Drunkards dream"
A very old specimen found in the
corner of a greenhouse

Homalocladium platycladium
"Ribbon bush" or "Tapeworm plant"

most interiors where the light is no weaker than the kind you can read by. Ideally suited for a dish garden planted with compatible plants (those that have about the same requirements), it is also attractive as a single potted subject for sill, greenhouse, or light garden. Mine spends spring and summer on a west window sill and then is put into the light garden at the far end of the tubes only when the daylength is shorter than nine hours. This plant was placed under the light in mid-November and started to bloom by mid-February at just about the same time as its greenhouse grown mother plant from which it was propagated as an offset. You will note that it has a much darker, intense green color when grown under lights than it has in the photograph taken of it in June after spending the last three months on an east window. Water/fertilize this gem only two days after the dipstick reads completely dry.

Homalocladium platycladium
"Ribbon bush" or "Tapeworm plant"

Often listed as an easy-to-grow plant, I wish someone would advise me about its actual requirements because no matter how I handled it, it invariably would develop brown-edged unattractive leaves. It also attracted white fly every time we opened the door nearby that leads to the street. It eventually wound up in the garden where it proceeded to die within a week.

73

Mikkelson

Sulfer inopurpur

Kalanchoe 'Rutkappchen'

Kalanchoe 'Korall'

Kalanchoe

These recent Mikklesen introductions from Europe now give you a wider choice of color and form. They can be grown in any interior space where it can be exposed to medium or stronger light. Small and compact in growing habit, these beauties should give you at least ten or more weeks of bloom during the winter months. Where space is limited such as in a small apartment, they are often used as a decorative plant in place of the Christmas traditional "Poinsettia". Even without their blossoms, they can be grown as small decorative accent plants in just about any place where people live and work. Water/fertilize only when the dipstick reads one third moist from the bottom. Though succulent in nature, you will find that they will require more frequent waterings than the other kinds.

Kalanchoe 'Saturn'

Kalanchoe 'Gelbe Melody'

Nopalxochia ackermanii
"Orchid cactus"

This epiphyte native of Mexico that normally is found growing at an altitude of from 6,000 to 8,000 feet has adapted to regular pot plant culture at sea level. It is particularly suited to growing in a raised planter or hanging basket because of its lax trailing habit. This plant has been in my neighbor's family for at least fifteen years. It is grown indoors in front of an east picture window and is summered outdoors on a west facing deck, starting after the last date of frost. This usually occurs around the fifteenth of May. And, it is brought back inside in the fall when the night temperatures start to consistently drop below 50°F. On an on demand water/fertilizing program, it is usually watered only after the soil is completely dry. This "Orchid cactus" comes into bloom at the beginning of July and will hold its bloom for at least two weeks.

Nopalxochia ackermanii
"Orchid cactus"

Nopalxochia ackermanii
"Orchid cactus"

75

Oscularia deltoides
"Pink fig marigold"

A blue-green creeping succulent that makes a fine pot plant or hanging basket for window sill or greenhouse culture. Although it prefers full light, it will adapt to light intensity as low as 500 foot candles (medium light). It is cold sensitive and prefers to be grown at a minimum of 65°F. Grown close up to the lights (four inches away) in the nursery shelf — it took off in all directions, and had to be kept within bounds by constant trimming. When grown in a hanging basket on an east window during the short days of winter, it just sat and sat while the parts closest to the window became chilled and proceeded to collapse. Given the proper care and culture it can be a useful, decorative plant and will provide good contrast to your others. Water/fertilize when the dipstick reads moist one half way up from the bottom if grown alone. Otherwise, it is adaptable to the once a week light garden schedule.

Pedilanthus tithymaloides variegatus
"Ribbon cactus", "Red bird" or "Devil's backbone"

One of my first choice interior plants. A medium to full light plant its green and white foliage will take on a pinkish hue and the plastic-appearing stems become a deeper green as the light intensifies. A slow grower, it can usually be grown in the same pot for a year or more. It can be increased by cuttings rooted in water or directly in the soil. Water/fertilize only two days after the dipstick reads dry.

Oscularia deltoides
Pink fig marigold

Pedilanthus tithymaloides variegatus
"Ribbon cactus" or "Red bird"
or "Devil's backbone"

PEPEROMIAS

If I were given a choice of only one family of plants to grow, I believe I'd choose the *Peperomias*. This easy-to-grow and easy-to-maintain family offers a very wide choice of shapes, forms, color, size and habit and, best of all, is widely distributed commercially. This family of plants will adapt satisfactorily to most any interior situation, require a minimum of maintenance, and will perform beautifully in low light and low humidity as well as in strong light and high humidity. Also, they will tolerate a wide range of temperatures without any observable effect. Mostly succulent in nature, they comply with one of my major maintenance requirements which is continuing to look well if I am not able to water them for a day or two after all signs indicate the need; that is, when the dipstick measures moist one quarter up from the bottom. Once these plants begin to bloom, they will continue to do so without let-up. True the blossoms are nothing to write home about but they do add interest.

Peperomia resedaeflora
"Mignonette peperomia"
One year later with
the last three months
in the light garden

I find that the thinner, quilted-leaved, multiple-crowned plants, such as *Peperomia caperata* "Emerald ripple", *Peperomia verschaffeltii* "Sweetheart peperomia", *Peperomia grisea argentea* "Ivy peromia," and *Peperomia resedaeflora* "Mignonette peperomia" with their compact, slow-growing habit are excellent subjects for low light situations, such as on a table or shelf that can be as far as ten feet from a window. They are also perfect subjects for end-of-tube growing in an artificial light garden. I have also observed that these

Peperomia resedaeflora
"Mignonette peperomia"
Sill grown

three kinds will start to bloom when the daylength is at least ten hours and will continue to do so year round during the longest days of summer as well as the shortest in winter. The easiest way to increase your plants of the aforementioned varieties is by breaking off the individual plants from the outer edge of the multiple crown and to pot them up immediately into the thoroughly moistened, regular growing medium.

As for the thicker, waxy-leaved varieties, such as *Peperomia obtusifolia* "Baby rubber plant" and *Peperomia magnoliaefolia* "Desert privet," I have yet to get them to bloom in any interior location. To bloom them, I suspect that these plants just like many garden geraniums require a certain amount of growth and maturity. Unfortunately for my plants, I do not allow them to produce sufficient growth to induce budding because I am continually propagating them for gifts and garden therapy projects.

The thick, waxy-leaved form as well as some of the trailing, thick-leaved kinds such as *Peperomia rubella* "Yerba Linda", *Peperomia orba* "Princess Astrid" and *Peperomia scandens* "Philodendron peperomia," are all prone to guttation, which means nothing more than the exudation of water from well-watered (after a thorough watering) plants on cool, moist nights that follow a warm day. This kind of reaction in no way affects the health or performance of a plant. This is a common occurrence among many kinds of plants including the Dieffenbachias. Guttation may be observed as droplets of water forming and dripping from around the edges of leaves or after taking stem cuttings when water seepage through the wound may continue as long as twenty-four hours before it begins to seal and callous. You can speed up the sealing process by dabbing each wound with some soil taken from the growing pot. This procedure is fine for most weeping plant wounds and is a common practice among commercial propagators of cacti and succulents.

Philodendron x 'Wend-imbe'

Philodendron x 'Wend-imbe'

Pilea depressa
"Miniature peperomia"
This two-year-old was moved
to a west window at
sixteen months and now has
some strands that hang
down as much as three feet.

Philodendron x "Wend-imbe"

Fine for medium to low light situations, it makes for a very decorative low floor plant or even a hanging basket. This is one of the "self heading" (forms multiple crowns) philodendrons that spreads out horizontally as it grows rather than climbs as the more well known kinds do. With the added interest in growing unusual philodendrons for decorating interior spaces, I'm sure that this plant will soon be widely distributed. Water/fertilize when dipstick is moist one half way up from bottom.

Pilea depressa "Miniature peperomia"

Another goody for the eclectic gardener. Although from my experience it prefers full light and temperatures of at least 65°F, I have also found that it will tolerate light as poor as that found five feet from a window and temperatures that go as low as 50°F. On a weekly water/fertilizing schedule, this is one of the most satisfying plants to grow. If you are in doubt about when to water, a dipstick moist one half way up from the bottom should serve as your guide.

Pilea depressa
"Miniature peperomia"
8-inch hanging basket about
one year old that
was moved to an east window
at eight months of age.

Peperomia magnoliaefolia
"Desert privet"
Sill grown

Peperomia orba
"Princess Astrid peperomia"
Sill grown — Two year old plant with the last six months under lights. It now has a two foot spread yet remains quite content in its five inch growing pot. It sits at the end of the tubes because of its space requirements. However, it does require a more intense light than is available in this situation. Yellowing leaves are the indicator. Therefore its pot sits atop an inverted plastic container so that the leaves almost touch the lights.

Peperomia magnoliaefolia
"Desert privet"
In 5-inch pot at one and a half years

Peperomia magnoliaefolia
"Desert Privet"
Same plant two years old after growing under lights for six months at the center of the tubes

Peperomia obtusifolia variegata
"Variegated peperomia"
Same plant two years old
after growing under light
for six months at the end
of the tubes

Peperomia obtusifolia variegata
"Variegated peperomia"
This one and a half year old plant was started
from a leaf cutting wherein the stem was inserted
down into the soil while the leaf part remained
above. Instead of rooting in two to three weeks when
started in water from regular joint cuttings, the
leaf cutting planted up in a thumb pot and placed in
the nursery took almost three months before
it showed any signs of growth. A slow starter, it quite
soon caught up with and soon overtook the
others. Grown under light from cutting to full grown
plant you can observe certain differences in
color and growing habit (weak stemmed and
trailing) than the mother plant of Peperomia
obtusifolia variegata and now can be considered a
clone of it. Thick leaved Peperomias with trailing
habit:

Peperomia obtusifolia variegata
"Variegated peperomia"
Sill grown

Peperomia obtusifolia
"Baby rubber plant"
Sill grown

Peperomia scandens
"Philodendron peperomia"

80

Peperomia verschaffeltii
"Sweetheart peperomia"
Sill grown — a very tiny mounding plant
that rarely attains a height of more than one
and a half inches above the soil line

Peperomia grisea argentea
"Ivy peperomia"
Sill grown

Peperomia caperata
"Emerald Ripple"
Sill grown

Platycerium ellisii
"Staghorn fern"

Polyscia fruticosa
"Ming aralia"
Hardwood rooted cutting

Platycerium ellisii
"Staghorn fern"

This smaller growing habit "Staghorn" has adapted beautifully to pot plant culture and to the kind of light available in the light garden. Normally an epiphyte that prefers to be grown attached to a piece of bark or a Sphagnum filled hanging basket, mine has adapted to a pot filled with one third regular potting soil and then topped with Sphagnum moss.

Always one to try new ideas especially when it comes to growing plants, I picked up the ripe banana feed idea from an educational exhibit about the care and culture of "Staghorns" at a flower show. Since my plants have been on a banana diet instead of the regular water/fertilizer, they have begun to grow and leaf out so that at this writing they are twice the size they were when photographed. All you do is share a banana with a plant by tucking thin slices including the skin under the first half inch of moss all around the pot. This also works for basket and bark grown plants. For these plants, slip thin slices of banana all around under the shield. Water down the moss so that it drips through the bottom of the pot drainage holes every time it feels dry to the touch. Ignore the tiny black fruit flies that may gather around the plant because of the enticing banana odor. They are not harmful and will soon disappear as the fruit disintegrates. Feed the plant with banana slices about every two weeks or after you observe that there is no sign of it.

Polyscia fruticosa
"Ming aralia"

Although the care and culture has been discussed on page 77 of *Houseplants and Indoor Landscaping,* I thought you might like to have an updating of my further experiences with this plant.

The plant now illustrated was purchased in early spring and was grown in a standard 4-inch pot on an east window until the following November. Due to excessive yellowing and leaf fall, it was placed under the center part of the lights in the rock garden where it soon recovered from the short day-length encountered on the window sill. By mid-February, it had grown up to the light and had begun to spread in all directions. It was at this time that I transplanted it into a regular bonsai pot and gave it a drastic pruning and potted up the pieces that had some mature (tan) wood. This kind of cutting usually roots fast. Green, soft wood cuttings usually take much longer to root and often rot out for me. This plant continues to enhance the light garden and has adapted to the once a week water/fertilizing program.

Polyscia fruticosa
"Ming aralia"
Pruned back for
bonsai training and
prunings

Polyscia fruticosa
"Ming aralia"
Three months under lights

Polyscia fruticosa
"Ming aralia"
Staging for home display or exhibit

Japanese style planter with plastic caps covering the drainage holes. I prefer to leave the caps in place rather than removing them as many growers do when they cover the inside bottom of the pot with plastic screening for soil retention and drainage. I find the caps just as effective.

Polyscias guilfoylei victoriae
"Lace aralia"

A delicate, lacy appearance belies this top performing plant. A slow grower, it meets all the requirements for an interior space plant for window, light garden or greenhouse growing. When grown alone, water/fertilize thoroughly when the dipstick reads moist two thirds up from the bottom.

Polyscias guilfoylei victoriae
"Lace aralia"
Pruned for bonsai training

Punica granatum nana
"Dwarf pomegranate"
With most of the soil removed from the root ball
and all long and/or broken roots removed
and pruned out to shape.

Punica granatum nana
"Dwarf pomegranate"
Grown under lights two months after it was root
pruned and shifted from a gallon can into a
four-inch pot.

Punica granatum nana
"Dwarf pomegranate"

Small in scale in every part, it is ideally suited for dwarfing and bonsai culture. An easy-to-grow-plant that will perform satisfactorily on an east, west or south window sill, it also makes for a light garden subject as well as any interior space where it can be exposed to full light. Where the climate permits, such as in California and Florida, or where night temperatures rarely drop below 35°F, this plant can be effectively used in low borders or as tubbed patio plants trained in the usual manner or as larger bonsais. For best results, water/fertilize thoroughly each time the dipstick indicates moist one half way up from the bottom.

Punica granatum nana
"Dwarf pomegranate"
Bonsai — after spreading a cover layer of growing
medium on the bottom of the pot about one
quarter (¼) inch deep, I set the plant and
previously selected lava rock in place, filled in the
soil all around the remaining spaces and to just below
the inside rim of the planter, watered it in
thoroughly, and set it back under the lights one
pot in from the end and to the side of the shelf. This
was done so that it would reach out to the light so that
all the branches and new growth would reach
out in one direction to the light to produce the
windswept bonsai style. Drastic pruning
of the roots as well as the above ground parts
apparently increases this plant's vigour because
within a month of transplant it had developed so
much new growth that I had to prune back
much of it to keep the plant in line. In fact, this
prune back has now become a bi-monthly chore.

85

Rhipsalis cereuscula
"Coral cactus"

Rhipsalis cereuscula
"Coral cactus"

Adaptable to most interior spaces that have at least 100 foot candles of light, this curious, slow growing succulent is most suitable for table, shelf, sill, light garden or even a cool greenhouse. Grown under optimum conditions (full diffused light), it will often send out erect branches that develop aerial roots. These branches soon become top heavy and will begin to trail out and over the pot seeking out a place to root down into. Therefore, in addition to making an exquisite pot plant it also is suitable for hanging baskets. Water/fertilize thoroughly after the dipstick is dry for two days.

Ruellia makoyana
"Monkey plant"

I was led to believe that this was a low spreading plant. Instead, it is an ungainly, tall-growing thin-branched plant that is redeemed by its foliage and free-flowering habit. Also, it makes good filler material for the flower arranger. It will take drastic pruning (to keep it within bounds) and will root in water or in soil with no apparent set-back. Moisture sensitive, it must be water/fertilized whenever the top of the soil feels dry to the touch. It prefers medium to full diffused light and the kind of humidity and temperature associated with a warm greenhouse or light garden.

Saintpaulia
"African Violets"

Basic care and culture has been discussed on pages 59 and 60 in *Houseplants and Indoor Landscaping.* However, in the short time since this was written, a number of new prolific blooms have been introduced nationally that I think you should know about. They are Ballet Violet Erica, Ballet Violet Karla, Ballet Violet Lisa, and Ballet Violet Meta. All are top performers and will adapt satisfactorily to medium diffused light, sill, greenhouse, and light garden culture. Most "Violet" growers have found best growing and blooming of plants is obtained in an all "Violet" garden where the same controlled conditions are available to all. Although most growers recommend at least twelve hours of artificial light, I do know a botanist who has attained equally good results with a mere six hours of artificial light. Another biologist friend is strictly an east window grower who uses the hydroponic method with excellent results. (See the chapter "Hydroponics.")

Their beauty should not be relegated only to their regular growing place. A change of climate for a few hours or even a few days will not be that harmful to them. Bring your plants out and display them for all to enjoy.

Ruellia makoyana
"Monkey plant"

3-tiered light unit filled with
Saintpaulia "African Violets"

Ballet Violets, Lisa (left) and Meta

Ballet Violet, Erica

Ballet Violet, Karla

Schefflera arborcola
"Dwarf schefflera"
Pruned out plant and soil
decorated with rock and cork to scale
and grown as a bonsai

Schefflera arborcola
"Dwarf schefflera"
One-year-old plant grown on an east window for
at least six months

Schefflera arborcola
"Dwarf schefflera"

A rather recent introduction to my "easy-to-grow" collection, I find that it is a slow grower and a minimum care plant. It will tolerate most interior growing conditions and adapt to light as poor as that available for reading (50-100 foot candles). My year old plant appears to be happiest when grown in the light garden where it has recently joined the other tropicals being trained as bonsais.

When grown alone, water/fertilize when the dipstick reads damp one fourth of the way up from the bottom.

Sedum lineare 'Variegatum'
"Carpet sedum"

Schefflera arborcola
"Dwarf schefflera"
Shifted to a bonsai growing pot, you will note
that it is set off center and tilted so that it will bend
in one direction. Tools are small enough to
work around soil and roots. Cuticle scissors are
sharp and make sharp cuts close up to the
trunk so that there is very little twig die back.

Sedum lineare 'Variegatum'
"Carpet sedum"

A hardy, succulent bedding plant that has adapted to indoor culture and is one of the so-called "new" introductions that you should be on the lookout for. It prefers the full light available on a west window, in a greenhouse or up as close as four inches away from the center part of the tubes in a light garden.

A few small pieces pressed gently in the growing medium will quickly root and start the slow, creeping growth that will completely cover the top of the soil with its tiny green and white leaves. Eventually, they will begin to trail over the rim of the pot to form a charmer that can be grown as a hanging basket. When grown alone, water/fertilize when the dipstick is moist one third up from the bottom.

Senecio herreianus (Kleinia gomphophylla)
"Green marble plant"
To increase your plants, snip off a string
long enough to encircle the inside of the pot a few
times. Press it down onto the pre-moistened
growing medium and set it into a tray with other
nursery plants, either on a sill or in a light
garden. Shift up to a larger pot when the strings of
beads begin to trail over the sides of the pots.
Wrap the trailing ends back up and press into the
soil so that these new parts will also root.
Continue the pot up and root procedure until
such time as your plants have covered the soil in the
final growing size pot you want. Now let
it wander where it will.

Selaginella kraussiana (denticulata)
"Trailing Irish moss" or "Club moss"

Senecio articulatus
(Kleinia articulata)
"Candle plant" or
"Candle cactus"

Selaginella kraussiana (denticulata)
"Trailing Irish moss" or "Club moss"

A plant for all spaces from light as poor as 50 foot candles to the year round full sun and light available at an unobstructed east window. Delicate and weak in appearance, it will stand up and perform better than most plants I've known and grown. It is so prolific that, grown among a collection of plants, its spores will take hold atop the soil and, if left to grow, will soon form a lush green mat. A most suitable indoor ground cover, it is starting to take hold on some of the Bonsai plantings and will make a most attractive replacement for the velvet, green moss that is usually used. It should be watered/fertilized on demand when grown alone. Depending on size of pot, time of year, and amount of humidity surrounding it, this may occur once a week or as infrequently as once a month. In the event that the plant starts to turn tan and appears to dry and fade, don't dump it. It is just resting and is preparing itself for its next spurt of growth. Water when the dipstick is moist one half way up from the bottom.

Senecio articulatus (Kleinia articulata)
"Candle plant" or "Candle cactus"

A very easy plant to grow, its rather rapid growth can be kept under control by removing any extra jointed stems that detract from the style of plant you would like to produce. I usually take out all the new mature growth that develops at the soil, which has a tendency to trail over the pot, and retain one or

Senecio herreianus (Kleinia gomphophylla)
"Green marble plant"
This one-and-a-half-year-old four-foot-long
stranded plant was started in the light garden and
has been growing in the same container on a
west window for one year. The more I snip it
for give-aways, the more it grows.

Senecio herreianus (Kleinia gomphophylla)
"Green marble plant"
Close up of strings and flowers that come
into bloom around the beginning of May and
persist as white feathery brushes after they're
dried. I've also noted that this plant and
others like it will throw sparse bloom through most
of the summer and on into early fall.

two strong main stems that branch out to form a miniature tree. Of course, the cuttings are potted up for growing on and eventual gifting. If I don't have the time to pot them up, they are stuck in a glass of water and set on a sill for display and eventual rooting. A full light plant, it will adapt to sill culture as well as the light garden. Moisture sensitive, its leaves shrivel and drop if the soil is permitted to dry out completely. For best results water/fertilize when the dipstick reads moist one half way up from the bottom.

Senecio herreianus (Kleinia gomphophylla)
"Green marble plant"

Properly grown, this people-stopper and door-bell-ringer is another of those easy-to-grow plants that will tolerate and adapt to most any interior space situation that is no more than five feet from an open uncurtained west or east window.

This creeping succulent's pointed ball-like leaves have translucent stripes known as "windows" which permit light for growth to reach the chlorophyll inside. These "windows" were developed as a protection against the intense heat and light that is typical of its native habitat in South Africa.

Its adaptation to interior space culture is so complete that it now prefers a water/fertilizing every time the dipstick is moist only one half way up from the bottom. If in doubt, observe the "beads". When there is insufficient moisture, they will turn to a lighter green and some may pop from the strings.

Sequoia sempervirens
*"Redwood tree" or "California redwood"
or "Coast redwood"*

Sequoia sempervirens
"Redwood tree" or California redwood" or "Coast redwood"

I always thought it was a "come on" — when I saw these burls offered for sale via mail order or in the retail shops. However, I now know it can be an easy plant to grow and show. See the chapter "Windowless Gardening" for care and culture of this burl chopped from the trunk of a "Redwood" growing in Medford, Oregon.

Setcreasea purpurea
"Purple heart"

Adapts to and tolerates most interior spaces where available light is strong enough to read by. A lusty large grower, its beautiful purple coloration and minimum maintenance warrants giving it growing space. The stronger the light, the more intense the color. You can keep it within bounds by breaking off pieces at the nodes. These pieces will root in water and in the growing medium in as little as three days. This is another plant that a flower arranger can look to for that extra touch of color to complete a design.

It is also the kind of plant that will not suffer if you cannot water it a day or two after the soil has dried out. Of course for best results water/fertilize when the dipstick is damp one third up from the bottom.

Setcreasea purpurea
"Purple heart"

Sinningia speciosa
"Gloxinia Minuteman"
"Gloxinia Redstone"

These popular florist type "Gloxinias" are usually flowered (brought into bloom) from January and on into summer in a light of at least 2500 foot candles.

They can be started from seed or from the tubers that develop in mature plants. Adaptable to the average interior environment, they perform best when the night temperatures range from 65°-70°F and daytime temperatures as high as 80°-85°F. Since they do best in a humidity of at least 50%, they should be considered primarily for greenhouse and artificial light garden culture. To maintain blooming store-bought plants, water/fertilize whenever the soil feels dry to the touch.

For more information about the care and culture of all kinds of "Gloxinias" I suggest that you contact the Gloxinia Society mentioned in the chapter "Artificial Light Gardening".

Sinningia speciosa
"Gloxinia minuteman" or "Gloxinia redstone"

low light

Spathiphyllum 'Mauna Loa'
"White anthurrium"

This too is a flower arrangers plant. The shiny green foliage is always there for the picking. And, when in bloom, the white spathe flowers are there for cutting and arranging whenever the mood sends you.

Spathiphyllum 'Mauna Loa'
"White anthurrium"

93

Strobilanthes dyerianus
"Persian shield"

A plant formerly restricted to warm greenhouses, it has proven adaptable for full light situation interior spaces. The stronger the light, the more intense the color. In fact, every time we put the photo flood lamps on to photograph it, it would turn almost purple within a minute and afterwards start to fade back to its average silver and green growing color.

Growing under lights apparently keeps the plant compact and with little need to repot more than once in nine months from thumb pot to the three-inch size. Also it began to bloom at six months and continues to do so in the center of the nursery shelf. The largest leaf is no longer than two inches. Another plant taken from the original stock plant and started at the same time as mine is grown by my daughter on a west window that can really heat up on a summer day. This plant, true to the reports of others, is a rampant grower that is now about eight inches high with leaves at least six inches in length and is now being grown in a 5-inch pot. My 4-inch-tall plant grown under lights has adapted to the once a week water/fertilizing schedule whereas my daughter's plant is on a demand schedule and is water/fertilized when the dipstick is moist two thirds up from the bottom or when the leaves begin to show signs of curling. Although my daughter's plant is now one year old, it still has not set flower. Perhaps there is something special about growing and blooming certain plants under lights.

Strobilanthes dyerianus
"Persian shield"

Strobilanthes dyerianus
"Persian shield"

Common Name Index

African violets - 86-87
Air plant - 36, 39
Australian bush cherry - 67

Baby rubber plant - 15, 77, 80
Baseball plant - 68
Begonia 'Amy' - 48, 49
Begonia 'Beatrice Haddrell' - 46, 48
Begonia 'Improved Schwabenland Pink' - 47
Begonia rex 'Fairy' - 49
Begonia 'Schwabenland Red' - 46
Begonia 'Schwabenland Twinkles' - 47
Black leaf panamiga - 37
Blue gum - 66-67
Bold sword fern - 21
Bowtie-plant - 71

Cactus plant - 90
Calico hearts - 44
California redwood - 92
Calla lily begonia - 27, 46, 47
Candelabra aloe - 23
Candle plant - 90
Carpet sedum - 89
Christmas cactus - 21, 51, 52
Climbing fig - 70
Club moss - 90
Coast redwood - 92
Coleus Carefree Jade - 62
Coleus Carefree Scarlet - 62
Copper rose - 64, 65
Coral cactus - 86
Corn cob cactus - 68
Crape myrtle - 23
Creeping fig - 70

Dainty rabbit's-food - 64
Desert privet - 77, 79
Devil's backbone - 76
Dragon tree - 23
Dragon tree agave - 23
Drunkard's dream - 72-73
Dwarf hinokicypress - 61

Dwarf pomegranate - 85
Dwarf rose striped star - 50
Dwarf schefflera -88, 89

Emerald ripple - 77, 81

False heather - 63
Fluffy ruffles - 21

Gloxinia minuteman - 93
Gloxinia redstone - 93
Green marble plant - 13, 90-91

Heart leaf philodendron - 20

Indoor oats - 50
Ivy peperomia - 77, 81

Jade plant - 21, 23

Kalanchoe - 74-75

Lace aloe - 27, 44, 45
Lace aralia - 84
Lace flower vine - 65
Lacy tree Philodendron - 23
Lemon tree - 23

Maidenhair tree - 71
Martha Washington geranium - 30
Mignonette peperomia - 77
Ming aralia - 82, 83
Miniature peperomia - 13, 78
Monkey plant - 86

Orchid cactus - 52, 53, 75
Oxtongue - 71

Partridge-breast - 26, 44, 45
Peanut cactus - 51
Peppermint geranium - 13
Persian shield - 13, 94

Philodendron peperomia - 77, 80
Pink fig marigold - 76
Princess Astrid - 77, 79
Princess pine - 63
Purple heart - 15, 92

Queen's tears - 50

Rat tail cactus - 51
Red bird - 76
Redwood tree - 92
Ribbon bush - 72
Ribbon cactus - 76
Rieger begonia - 46
Rosary vine - 61
Rubber plant - 23

Schefflera - 22
Silver sheen - 30, 37, 39, 66
Spider aralia - 64
Staghorn fern - 82
Star window plant - 72
Strawberry begonia - 7
Strawberry geranium - 7, 37
String of hearts - 61
Sweetheart peperomia - 77, 81

Table fern - 13, 37
Tapeworm plant - 73
Tiger aloe - 26
Trailing Irish moss - 39, 90
Turkish temple - 68

Umbrella plant - 63

Variegated peperomia - 80
Variegated snake plant - 21

Weeping fig - 70
White anthurrium - 93
White poinsettia - 68-69

Yerba Linda - 77

Latin Name Index

Adromischus maculatus - 44
Aeonium archrichsym - 44, 45
Agave attenuata - 23
Aloe arboescens - 23
Aloe aristata - 27, 44, 45
Aloe variegata ausana - 26, 44, 45
Aporocactus flagelliformis - 51
Ariocarpus kotschubeyanus - 53, 60
Astrophytum asterias - 59
Astrophytum capricorne - 54
Astrophytum myriostigma - 55, 58
Astrophytum ornatum - 55

Begonia 'Amy' - 48, 49
Begonia 'Beatrice Haddrell' - 46, 48
Begonia 'Improved Schwabenland Pink' - 47
Begonia rex 'Fairy' - 49
Begonia 'Schwabenland Red' - 46
Begonia 'Schwabenland Twinkles' - 47
Begonia semperflorens albo-foliis - 27, 46, 47
Billbergia nutans - 50
Brassia actinophylla - 22

Cephalocereus palmerii - 55
Ceropegia woodii - 61

Chamaecerus silvestre - 51, 58
Chamaecyparis obtusa nana - 61
Coleus - 62
Crassula argentea - 21, 23
Crassula pseudolycopodioides - 63
Cryptanthus bivittatus minor - 50
Cuphea hyssopifolia - 63
Cyperus alternitolius - 63

Davallia fejeensis plumosa - 64
Dizygotheca elegantissima - 64
Dolichothele sphaerica - 60
Dracaena draco - 23

Echeveria multicaulis - 64, 65
Echinocereus cinerascens - 52
Echinocereus engelmannii - 59
Echinocereus pentalophus - 60
Echinocereus reichenbachii - 54
Echinocereus salm-dyckianus - 60
Echinocereus triglochidatus - 56
Episcia cuperata 'Silver Sheen' - 30, 37, 39, 66
Episcia dianthiflora - 65
Eucalyptus globulus - 66, 67
Eugenia myrtifolia - 67

Euphorbia mammillaris - 68
Euphorbia obesa - 68
Euphorbia pulcherrima 'Ecke's White' - 68-69

Ferocactus latispinus - 56, 60
Ficus benjamina - 70
Ficus decora - 23
Ficus pumila - 70
Ficus repens - 70

Gasteria x 'Hybrida' - 71
Gymnocalycium baldianum - 56
Gymnocalycium bruchii - 54
Gymnocalycium damsii - 53
Gymnocalycium denudatum - 53, 57
Gymnocalycium friedrickii - 53
Ginkgo biloba - 71

Hatiora salicornioides - 72-73
Haworthia cuspidata - 72
Homalocladium platycladium - 73

Kalanchoe 'Gelbe Melody' - 75
Kalanchoe inopurpur - 74
Kalanchoe 'Korall' - 74